content

It's easy to rave about a juicy steak or a decadent dessert, but a memorable salad is a real success. Ripe vegetables, crisp lettuce, colorful accents and flavorful dressings come together to make a truly exciting dish. Whether it's an accompaniment to a main dish or a filling alternative to a heavy dinner, salads are the ultimate vehicle for imaginative cooks.

The Healthy Salad on the Go container from Tupperware is the perfect way to take freshness along wherever your day leads. With three separate features, this product is a mobile salad bar, ready when you are.

The container sports a virtually airtight and liquid-tight seal so you don't have to worry about spills or spoilage. The seal houses an innovative snap-together fork and knife, and a small, virtually airtight and liquid-tight container nestles comfortably to house dressings that won't weigh your salad down. When you're ready to eat, drizzle the dressing over fresh greens for a refreshing and healthy lunch option.

This recipe book showcases 24 salads and 13 dressings for you to mix and match. From Thai-inspired combinations to pasta salads to satisfy, these fresh creations were designed with you and your family in mind. Bon appétit!

Baby Spinach
It's heralded as a healthy choice, but the dark green color and mild flavor of baby spinach is delicious, too.

Arugula
Peppery arugula has a long leaf and a forward flavor redolent of spices and herbs. It's a wonderful green to pair with sweet, fruity salads.

Romaine
Made famous by the classic caesar salad, romaine ranges from light green hearts to dark outer leaves that are full of crunch and fresh flavor.

Bibb
Soft and buttery, this lettuce provides an alternative to iceberg that showcases a salad's subtle sweetness.

Spring Mix
If you're going for bagged salad mix, this is the best way to go. A combination of flavors, colors and textures lend interest to the plate and excite the palate.

great greens

There's more to salad greens than plain, old iceberg. Try some new greenery, like spicy arugula or buttery Bibb, the next time you take your Healthy Salad on the Go.

Red Leaf
In dramatic maroon, red leaf lettuce adds a pop of color and to any plate, and is characterized by its mild flavor, similar to green leaf lettuce.

Green Leaf
Frilly leaves and an almost-sweet flavor make this lettuce a favorite among salad lovers. An excellent alternative to romaine or iceberg because of its neutrality.

Radicchio
The cabernet-colored radicchio is great on the grill, which brings out its sweet undertones. Mixed with other greens, radicchio offers a complex contrast.

Iceberg
Classic iceberg is crunchy, refreshing, and keeps well in the refrigerator for weeks, if properly stored.

Napa Cabbage
Long, wide, crinkled leaves and mild flavor characterize this member of the cabbage family.

Frisée (see pages 17–18)
This unique French lettuce has elegant feathery leaves, a slightly bitter flavor that pairs particularly well with creamy elements like egg yolk or velvety dressing.

side salads

You don't have to resort to one-note side dishes; these salads might just steal the show. A well-composed salad can add visual interest and complex flavor to a meal. Serving a memorable meal is as easy as combining fresh ingredients and exciting flavors with good nutrition. Put away the steamed broccoli for a night and prepare an easy and delicious salad instead.

spectacular side salads

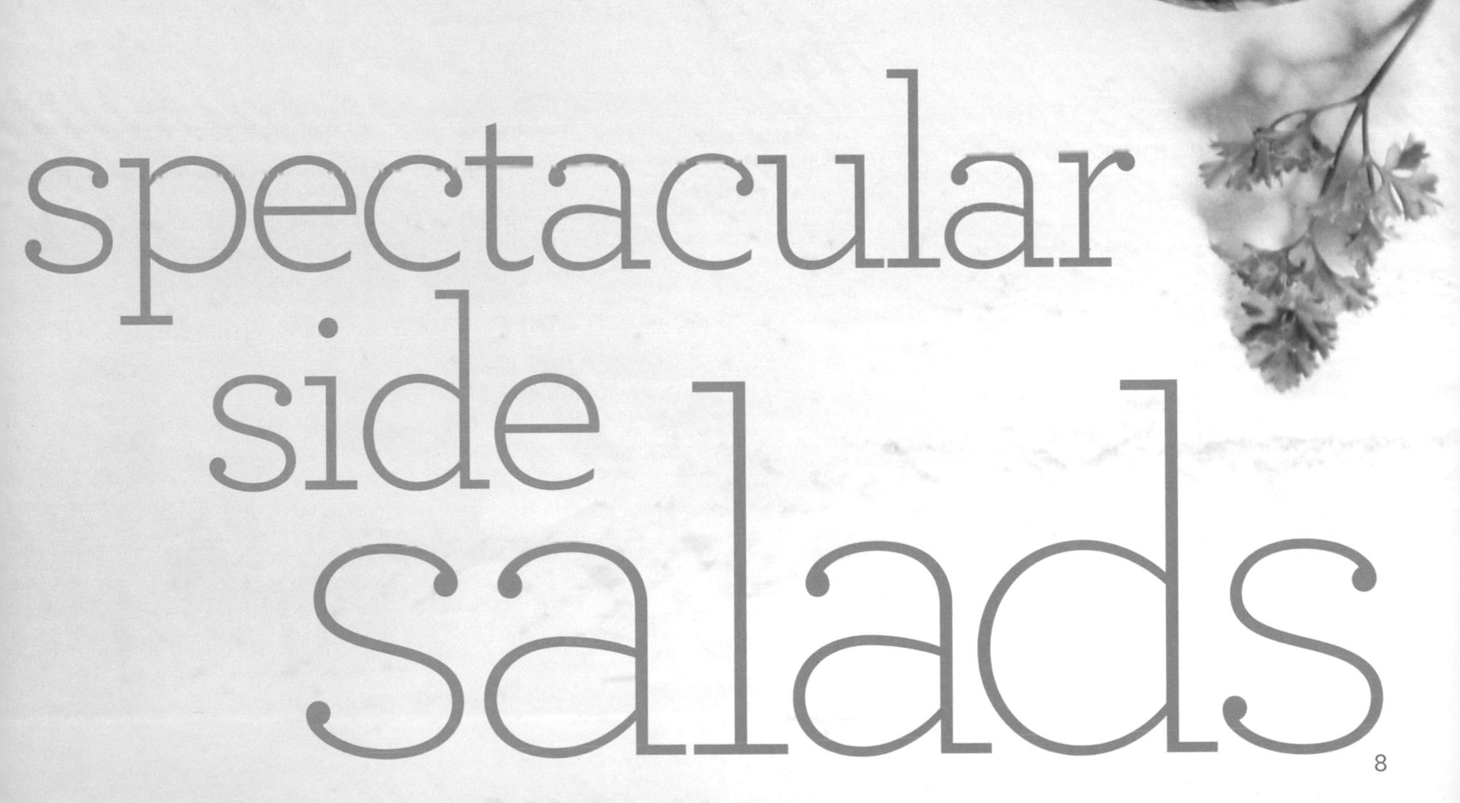

Serves 4

basmati rice

A delicious alternative to plain rice, this salad incorporates briny kalamata olives, corn and green onions for color and flavor sure to impress.

1 cup Basmati rice
2 cups water
1/3 cup canola oil
3 tbsp. white wine vinegar
1 tsp. Dijon mustard
1 tsp. honey
¼ tsp. dry ginger
1 cup cooked fresh or frozen corn
2 green onions, chopped
½ cup cashews, chopped
1 cup pitted Kalamata olives, chopped
salt and pepper

Combine the rice and 2 cups of water in a **Tupperware® Microwave Rice Maker.** Replace cover and microwave on high for 5 minutes. Then, microwave on medium for 15 minutes. Allow to sit 5 minutes. Fluff with a serving spoon and set aside.

To make the dressing, combine the oil, vinegar, mustard, honey and ginger in a **Quick Shake® Container**. Season with salt and pepper. Set aside.

To assemble the salad, combine the cooked rice, dressing and remaining ingredients in a large bowl. Toss together and serve warm, room temperature or cold.

Nutritional Information (per serving):
Calories: 250 Total Fat: 15g Saturated Fat: 1.5g Cholesterol: 0mg Carbohydrate: 28g Sugar: 1g Fiber: 2g Protein: 4g Sodium: 190mg Vitamin A: 3% Vitamin C: 5% Calcium: 3% Iron: 7%

Serves 4

caprese

Serve this light salad in the summer when tomatoes and basil are both at the peak of freshness.

8 oz./225 g fresh mozzarella, in water
6 small vine-ripe tomatoes
Basil Vinaigrette (see page 63)
½ cup fresh basil leaves
salt and pepper

Using a **Chef Series™ Pro Serrated Utility Knife**, cut the tomatoes into slices. Slice fresh mozzarella into rounds. Place tomato slices, fresh basil and mozzarella in a layered stack to serve. Drizzle with Basil Vinaigrette and season with salt and pepper to taste.

Note: Leftover Caprese Salad can be added to pasta or mixed with salad greens for a salad.

Nutritional Information (per serving):
Calories: 470 Total Fat: 41g Saturated Fat: 11g Cholesterol: 45mg Carbohydrate: 13g Sugar: 10g Fiber: 2g Protein: 14g Sodium: 360mg Vitamin A: 40% Vitamin C: 30% Calcium: 30% Iron: 6%

Serves 6

ceviche veracruz

This Mexican-style ceviche is delicious for an outdoor picnic or barbecue, offering a lighter complement to grilled meats.

1 lb./455 g shrimp, peeled and deveined (tails removed)
juice of 2 lemons
juice of 2 limes
juice of 2 oranges
1 cucumber, seeded and peeled
½ cup red onion, peeled and chopped
2 jalapeño peppers, seeded
1 tomato, seeded
1 avocado, pitted
¼ cup cilantro
salt and pepper

Toss shrimp with half citrus juices and place in **Tupperware® SmartSteamer.** Fill Water Tray with 1¾ cups water. Microwave on high for 7 minutes. Remove from microwave, place shrimp in the **Quick Chef**, fitted with blade attachment, and chop coarsely. Transfer to a large bowl. Add remaining citrus juices to the bowl. Set aside.

Place cucumber, onion and pepper in base of the **Quick Chef** and chop coarsely. Transfer to the bowl with shrimp. Place the tomato, avocado and cilantro in base of the **Quick Chef** and turn handle to chop coarsely. Add to the bowl. Stir to combine ingredients, season to taste. Serve with tortilla chips if desired.

Nutritional Information (per serving):
Calories: 150 Total Fat: 6g Saturated Fat: 1g Cholesterol: 110mg Carbohydrate: 11g Sugar: 5g Fiber: 3g Protein: 14g Sodium: 135mg Vitamin A: 10% Vitamin C: 60% Calcium: 4% Iron: 10%

Serves 4

greek with warm pita crisps

The perfect combination of high-quality, fresh ingredients is what has leant this salad its longevity. Pita chips are perfect for scooping up that last cube of feta cheese.

4 pieces pita bread, quartered
½ tsp. dried oregano
1 tsp. extra virgin olive oil
10 oz./285g romaine salad greens
1 cucumber
1 tomato
1 cup black olives
2 green onions
½ cup Greek Dressing (see page 63)
¾ cup crumbled feta cheese

Preheat oven to 350° F/175° C.

Place the pita on a baking sheet. Drizzle the bread with olive oil. Sprinkle with dried oregano, salt and pepper. Place in the oven for 10 minutes, or until the pita is crisp.

While pita is toasting, assemble the salad. Add cucumber, tomato, black olives and green onions to the base of the **Quick Chef**. Turn handle to coarsely chop. Combine the salad greens, cucumber, tomato, olives and green onion. Toss with ¼ cup dressing. Top with the cheese and warm pita. Serve immediately.

Nutritional Information (per serving):
Calories: 280 Total Fat: 16g Saturated Fat: 4g Cholesterol: 10mg Carbohydrate: 27g Sugar: 3g
Fiber: 6g Protein: 10g Sodium: 830mg Vitamin A: 140% Vitamin C: 45% Calcium: 15% Iron: 15%

Serves 6

parisian bistro

This salad is très française, and something you can find in bistros all over Paris. Bitter frisée is complemented by the tangy goat cheese and creamy poached egg.

1 baguette (French bread), cut into 20 slices
5 oz./140 g chèvre goat cheese
1 head frisée lettuce
½ cup chopped walnuts
black pepper
6 eggs, poached or fried
Sizzlin' Vinaigrette (see page 67)

Preheat broiler. Slice baguette with **Chef Series™ Pro Bread Knife**. Use a **Chef Series™ Pro Paring Knife** to cut the goat cheese into thin slices. Place one slice of cheese on each bread slice to make a crouton. Sprinkle with black pepper, if desired. Place under broiler and broil until cheese turns golden. Place frisée leaves on salad plates, top with egg, 2–3 croutons and sprinkle with walnuts.

Nutritional Information (per serving):
Calories: 590 Total Fat: 40g Saturated Fat: 6g Cholesterol: 45mg Carbohydrate: 45g Sugar: 3g
Fiber: 5g Protein: 16g Sodium: 950mg Vitamin A: 45% Vitamin C: 10% Calcium: 10% Iron: 20%

Serves 5

quinoa & black bean

Quinoa is a whole-grain and a good source of protein and amino acids that can help with immune system function and overall health. The subtle fragrance of orange gives this special side salad added elegance.

1 cup quinoa
1½ cups fat-free chicken broth
½ cup fresh squeezed orange juice
1 tbsp. grated orange zest
⅓ cup extra virgin olive oil
2 cloves garlic, minced
juice of one lime
¼ cup cilantro, chopped
1 tbsp. Dijon mustard
1 tbsp. Simple Indulgence™ Southwest Chipotle Seasoning Blend
1 small yellow pepper, quartered
2 medium vine-ripened tomatoes, chopped
15 oz./425 g can black beans, drained
1 small red pepper, seeded and cut into large chunks
salt and pepper

Combine quinoa, chicken broth, orange juice and zest in a **Tupperware® Microwave Rice Maker**. Replace cover and microwave on high for 15–18 minutes. Fluff with a serving spoon. Place olive oil, garlic, lime juice, cilantro, Dijon mustard and Seasoning Blend in a **Quick Shake® Container**. Replace seal and shake well to combine. Place red and yellow peppers in base of **Chop 'N Prep™ Chef**. Replace cover and pull cord 2–3 times to coarsely chop. Place peppers and remaining ingredients with cooked quinoa in a large bowl. Toss vegetables and cooked quinoa with dressing. Season with salt and pepper to taste.

Nutritional Information (per serving):
Calories: 340 Total Fat: 17g Saturated Fat: 2.5g Cholesterol: 30mg Carbohydrate: 40g Sugar: 7g Fiber: 6g Protein: 10g Sodium: 610mg Vitamin A: 2% Vitamin C: 40% Calcium: 4% Iron: 15%

Serves 4

spinach & pear

If you fancy blue cheeses, go for the good stuff. Maytag and Danish blues are some of the best, and a little goes a long way.

1 package baby spinach leaves
2 Anjou pears, peeled, cored and sliced
½ cup walnut halves
½ cup Gorgonzola or bleu cheese crumbles
Poppy Seed Dressing (see page 65)

Place spinach and pears in a large bowl. Place nuts in base of the **Quick Chef**. Replace cover and turn handle to coarsely chop. Add to spinach and sliced pears. Sprinkle cheese over salad. Drizzle dressing on top and toss lightly to combine.

Nutritional Information (per serving):
Calories: 340 Total Fat: 23g Saturated Fat: 5g Cholesterol: 25mg Carbohydrate: 31g Sugar: 19g Fiber: 6g Protein: 8g Sodium: 630mg Vitamin A: 120% Vitamin C: 40% Calcium: 20% Iron: 15%

Serves 4

strawberry & spinach

Strawberries are best during March-August, so this salad is a fantastic mid-summer night's treat. Sliced, grilled chicken, tofu or steak takes this salad from side story to main event.

½ lb. sliced strawberries
10 oz./285 g baby spinach
4 oz./115 g crumbled goat cheese
2 tbsp. pine nuts, toasted
Honey Mustard Dressing (see page 63)

In a medium bowl, combine strawberries and baby spinach. Sprinkle with crumbled goat cheese and toasted pine nuts. Drizzle with your favorite dressing.

Nutritional Information (per serving):
Calories: 190 Total Fat: 13g Saturated Fat: 7g Cholesterol: 30mg Carbohydrate: 8g Sugar: 4g
Fiber: 3g Protein: 12g Sodium: 150mg Vitamin A: 130% Vitamin C: 90% Calcium: 35% Iron: 15%

Serves 8

summer fresh fruit

A small spoonful of real whipped cream makes all the difference in this island version of fruit salad. Almonds and flaked coconut add exotic flavor and crunch.

2 cups cantaloupe
2 cups watermelon
1 lb./455 g strawberries, stems removed
2 kiwis, peeled
1 cup heavy cream
2 tbsp. superfine sugar
1 tsp. rum extract, optional
½ cup flaked coconut, toasted
½ cup sliced almonds, toasted

With **Chef Series™ Pro Chef's Knife**, cut all fruit and place in a medium bowl. Place heavy cream in the base of the **Whip 'N Prep™ Chef**; replace cover and turn handle to whip until cream begins to thicken. Add sugar and extract, and beat until stiff peaks form. Sprinkle with coconut and almonds; top with whipped cream. Serve immediately.

Nutritional Information (per serving):
Calories: 240 Total Fat: 16g Saturated Fat: 9g Cholesterol: 40mg Carbohydrate: 23g Sugar: 16g Fiber: 4g Protein: 4g Sodium: 20mg Vitamin A: 45% Vitamin C: 170% Calcium: 6% Iron: 6%

Serves 6

surf's up shrimp

Inspired by a trip to Hawaii, this salad is a mixture of land and sea, combining tropical flavors for a unique experience.

1 lb./455 g cooked shrimp, peeled and deveined
1 pineapple, peeled, cored and cut into chunks
2 mangoes, peeled and cut into chunks
2 bananas, sliced
1 tbsp. shredded coconut, toasted
1 tbsp. cashews, toasted and chopped
2 tbsp. canola oil
2 tbsp. brewed coffee
1 tbsp. low-sodium soy sauce
1 lime, zested and juiced
2 tbsp. light coconut milk
1 habañero pepper, seeded
½ cup cilantro, chopped
1 tsp. fresh ginger, minced
salt and pepper

6 cups arugula, optional

Place shrimp, pineapple, mangoes, bananas, coconut and cashews in a large bowl. Toss to combine. Add oil, coffee, soy sauce, lime juice and coconut milk to the base of a **Quick Shake® Container** and set aside. Place habañero pepper, cilantro and ginger in **Chop 'N Prep™ Chef** and pull cord 4-5 times or until finely chopped. Add mixture to **Quick Shake® Container**, replace cover and shake until well combined. Pour dressing over shrimp and fruit and chill in refrigerator at least 1 hour. Serve over arugula, if desired.

Nutritional Information (per serving):
Calories: 290 Total Fat: 7g Saturated Fat: 1g Cholesterol: 145mg Carbohydrate: 43g Sugar: 30g Fiber: 5g Protein: 18g Sodium: 240mg Vitamin A: 20% Vitamin C: 180% Calcium: 6% Iron: 20%

Salads can be satisfying. Try one of these main dish marvels. Combine crisp lettuces with colorful fruits and vegetables and add a good source of protein for a filling salad that won't leave you feeling sluggish. Add nutrient-rich beans, tofu, pork, steak, fish or chicken to almost any salad for a main dish to inspire the senses.

main dish salads

Serves 8

bombay mango chicken

Smoky curry and bursts of fresh mango complement the earthy qualities of this fantastic version of classic chicken salad.

⅓ cup non-fat plain Greek yogurt
⅓ cup low-fat mayonnaise
1 tbsp. curry powder
3 tbsp. lime juice
1 tbsp. honey
3 cooked chicken breasts (poached or steamed in the **Tupperware® SmartSteamer**), diced
1 ripe mango, peeled, pitted and chopped
1 cup red seedless grapes, halved
8 oz./225 g can water chestnuts, drained
½ cup salted, roasted cashews
salt and pepper

In your favorite large bowl or **Whip 'N Prep™ Chef**, whisk together the yogurt, mayonnaise, curry powder, lime juice and honey. Add the remaining ingredients and gently combine with the dressing. Serve immediately or refrigerate for up to three days.

Nutritional Information (per serving):
Calories: 190 Total Fat: 8g Saturated Fat: 1.5g Cholesterol: 30mg Carbohydrate: 17g Sugar: 11g Fiber: 2g Protein: 13g Sodium: 120mg Vitamin A: 4% Vitamin C: 20% Calcium: 2% Iron: 8%

Serves 6

cashew chicken lettuce cups

The crunch of fresh lettuce complements creamy cashews and authentic Asian flavors in these fun-to-eat lettuce wraps.

1 head iceberg or Bibb lettuce
3 chicken breasts (poached or steamed in **Tupperware® SmartSteamer**)
1 tsp. sesame oil
½ yellow onion, chopped
1-inch piece fresh ginger
6 garlic cloves
¾ cup hoisin sauce
5 tbsp. soy or tamari sauce
1 tsp. sweet chili sauce
1 cup cashews, chopped

To prepare lettuce cups, separate the outer leaves from the head of lettuce, using care not to break the leaves. Wash, pat dry and set on a serving plate. Chop the chicken breasts into small chunks. Set aside.

In a **Chef Series™ 11"/28 cm Fry Pan with Cover**, heat the sesame oil over medium heat. In the meantime, chop the onion, ginger and garlic in a **Quick Chef**. Add the mixture to the pan and cook 5 minutes, until vegetables are tender. Add the chicken, cashews, hoisin sauce, soy sauce and chili sauce. Stir and cook until heated through. Serve immediately with lettuce, allowing everyone to assemble the lettuce wraps themselves.

Nutritional Information (per serving):
Calories: 300 Total Fat: 14g Saturated Fat: 2.5g Cholesterol: 40g Carbohydrate: 27g Sugar: 13g Fiber: 3g Protein: 20g Sodium: 1490mg Vitamin A: 10% Vitamin C: 8% Calcium: 6% Iron: 15%

Serves 8

orzo & baby spinach

The fresh pesto in this salad makes all the difference, adding nutty depth and verdant color to the salad. Make the pesto a day ahead to let flavors harmonize.

Pesto Sauce (see page 65)
Pesto Vinaigrette (see page 65)
2 cups uncooked orzo pasta
2 cups cooked chicken (either made in the **Tupperware® SmartSteamer** or rotisserie)
8 oz./225 g cherry tomatoes
6 oz./170 g baby spinach, washed
2–3 tbsp. shredded Parmesan cheese
salt and pepper

Bring 2 Qts./1.8 L salted water to a boil in a **Chef Series™ 3-Qt./2.8 L Saucepan**. Add orzo pasta and cook 9 minutes or until *al dente*. Drain pasta, toss with spinach, chicken, tomatoes and Pesto Vinaigrette. Add Parmesan cheese, salt and pepper to taste.

Nutritional Information (per serving):
Calories: 430 Total Fat: 24g Saturated Fat: 4g Cholesterol: 35mg Carbohydrate: 34g Sugar: 3g Fiber: 2g Protein: 19g Sodium: 105mg Vitamin A: 50% Vitamin C: 15% Calcium: 8% Iron: 15%

Serves 4

quinoa & pork tenderloin

Quinoa is a grain from Peru with a similar texture to couscous. It is readily available in most grocery stores and is a delicious way to add whole grains to your diet.

2 lb./1kg pork tenderloin
5.6 oz./160 g pkg. plain, uncooked quinoa
½ cup sliced, marinated artichoke hearts
¼ cup sliced olives
½ bunch fresh baby spinach
1 cup cherry tomatoes, cut in half
2 tbsp. flat-leaf parsley, finely chopped
¼ cup balsamic vinegar
1½ tbsp. extra virgin olive oil
4 cloves garlic, minced
salt and pepper

Place water in Water Tray of **Tupperware® Smart Steamer**. Place pork tenderloin in base. Microwave on high power 17 minutes, or until the pork tenderloin reaches an internal temperature of 165° F / 74° C. Let rest 5 minutes, then slice thinly.

Prepare quinoa in the **Tupperware® Microwave Rice Maker** according to the directions in the product insert. Allow to cool and fluff with a serving spoon. Add artichoke hearts, olives, spinach, cherry tomatoes and parsley. In a small bowl, whisk together balsamic vinegar, olive oil and garlic until well blended; season with salt and pepper to taste and pour over salad. Stir to combine.

Nutritional Information (per serving):
Calories: 620 Total Fat: 26g Saturated Fat: 6g Cholesterol: 150mg Carbohydrate: 36g Sugar: 7g Fiber: 5g Protein: 57g Sodium: 290mg Vitamin A: 90% Vitamin C: 40% Calcium: 10% Iron: 35%

Serves 4

santa fe chicken with quesadillas

Enjoy zesty Tex-Mex flavor in this south-of-the-border salad the whole family will love.

- 10 oz./285 g bagged mixed salad greens
- 15 oz./425 g can black beans, drained
- 1 cup frozen corn
- 2 chicken breasts
- 1 tsp. vegetable oil
- 4 8-inch flour tortillas
- 1 cup shredded sharp cheddar cheese
- ½ cup Cilantro-Lime Vinaigrette (see page 63)
- salt and pepper

In the **Tupperware® SmartSteamer**, place the chicken in the Steamer Base and the frozen corn in the Colander. Fill the Water Tray with 1½ cups/400 mL water. Microwave on high for 15 minutes or until the chicken is cooked through. When cool enough to handle, slice the chicken into thin slices. Set aside.

Heat the vegetable oil in a **Chef Series™ 8"/20 cm Fry Pan** over medium-high heat. Place ¼ cup of the cheese on one side of each tortilla. Fold the tortilla in half and then place in the pan, cooking in batches. Cook for 2 minutes on each side, until cheese is melted and exterior of tortilla is golden. Set aside and keep warm.

In a serving bowl, toss the mixed greens, corn, beans, chicken and prepared dressing together. Top with the quesadillas. Serve immediately.

Nutritional Information (per serving):
Calories: 540 Total Fat: 24g Saturated Fat: 8g Cholesterol: 65mg Carbohydrate: 51g Sugar: 4g Fiber: 8g Protein: 30g Sodium: 1520mg Vitamin A: 60% Vitamin C: 8% Calcium: 25% Iron: 80%

Serves 4

steakhouse

Take a trip to your favorite steakhouse just by making this easy, delicious salad. This hearty main dish is sure to satisfy even the biggest appetites.

2 4 oz./115 g filet mignon steaks
2 large portobello mushrooms, sliced
1 tsp. vegetable oil
10 oz./265 g bagged mixed salad greens
½ cup Raspberry Red Wine Vinaigrette (see page 65)
½ cup bleu cheese crumbles
½ cup jarred roasted red peppers, drained and sliced
salt and pepper

In a **Chef Series™ 11"/28 cm Fry Pan**, heat the oil over medium-high heat. Season the steaks with salt and pepper, and then place in the hot pan, searing for 6 minutes on each side or until steak reaches desired degree of doneness. Remove steaks and allow to rest on a cutting board 5 minutes. Cook mushrooms in hot oil until tender. Remove mushrooms. Carve meat into thin slices. Keep warm.

To assemble salad, place salad greens in a large bowl. Toss with the dressing. Top with meat, mushrooms, peppers and cheese. Serve immediately.

Nutritional Information (per serving):
Calories: 410 Total Fat: 35g Saturated Fat: 9g Cholesterol: 50mg Carbohydrate: 9g Sugar: 4g Fiber: 3g Protein: 17g Sodium: 410mg Vitamin A: 60% Vitamin C: 15% Calcium: 10% Iron:10%

series Pro

Serves 4

steamed salmon & asian slaw

This Asian-inspired salad combines all the things that make Asian food exciting: sweet, salty, sour and earthy. Salmon is full of monounsaturated fats that keep you healthy and lower cholesterol.

1 lb./455 g salmon filet
2 lb. head Napa cabbage
1 bunch green onions
1 pkg. ramen noodles
1 pkg. slivered or sliced almonds
3 tbsp. butter
salt and pepper
Sweet & Sour Dressing (see page 67)

Steam salmon for 10 minutes in **Tupperware® SmartSteamer** until opaque. Thinly chop cabbage and slice green onions and place in a large bowl. Heat butter in a **Chef Series™ 11"/28 cm Fry Pan** over medium heat. Crush noodles and add with almonds to melted butter. Cook until golden brown. Drain well and set aside. Just before serving, add noodles and almonds to cabbage and toss with dressing. Top with steamed salmon.

Nutritional Information (per serving):
Calories: 920 Total Fat: 63g Saturated Fat: 10g Cholesterol: 95mg Carbohydrate: 56g Sugar: 30g Fiber: 9g Protein: 38g Sodium: 310mg Vitamin A: 60% Vitamin C: 110% Calcium: 30% Iron: 15%

Serves 4

thai beef & tofu

Fresh herbs and lots of crunch make this salad sparkle. Add Mandarin orange segments for a touch a sweetness.

12 oz./340 g extra firm tofu
6 cups spring mix salad greens
½ cup fresh mint
½ cup fresh basil
1 large cucumber, peeled and sliced thickly
1 red onion, quartered
1 tbsp. peanut oil
8 oz./225 g skirt or flank steak, trimmed
8 oz./225 g can Mandarin orange segments, drained
salt and pepper
Thai Dressing (see page 67)

Line a plate with paper towels. Remove the tofu from packaging, drain and cut into 1-inch cubes. Set tofu cubes on paper towels and allow to drain for 30 minutes. Gently press out any remaining liquid from tofu cubes using additional paper towels.

In **Quick Chef** fitted with the blade attachment, combine onion and cucumber and turn handle to chop coarsely. In a large bowl, combine lettuce, mint, basil and the cucumber mixture. Pour half of the vinaigrette over the lettuce mixture; toss to coat. Heat **Chef Series™ 11"/ 28 cm Fry Pan** over medium-high heat. Add peanut oil to pan. Add beef and cook for 3 minutes per side or until meat reaches desired degree of doneness. Remove meat from pan and allow to rest 5 minutes on a cutting board. Add tofu to hot pan. Cook tofu until lightly browned. Remove from heat and set aside. Slice beef thinly and place in bowl with lettuce mixture. Add tofu; toss to combine. Top with orange segments.

Note: Substitute steamed chicken or salmon for the beef.

Nutritional Information (per serving):
Calories: 270 Total Fat: 15g Saturated Fat: 2.5g Cholesterol: 30mg Carbohydrate: 15g Sugar: 7g Fiber: 4g Protein: 22g Sodium: 400mg Vitamin A: 35% Vitamin C: 45% Calcium: 25% Iron: 25%

Serves 4

turkey cobb

There are few things better than a classic Cobb. This main-dish salad combines all the vintage trimmings with an elegant champagne vinaigrette.

2 tbsp. champagne vinegar
2 tsp. Dijon mustard
1 tsp. Worcestershire sauce
½ cup light mayonnaise
¼ cup extra virgin olive oil
4 oz./115 g crumbled bleu cheese
¾ cup or 6 slices pre-cooked bacon, crumbled
10 oz./285 g spring mix salad greens
1 small avocado peeled, pitted and sliced
4 small tomatoes, chopped
½ lb. turkey breast, cubed
salt and pepper

In base of **Whip 'N Prep™ Chef**, place champagne vinegar, Dijon mustard, Worcestershire sauce, mayonnaise and olive oil. Replace cover and turn handle to thoroughly mix. Set aside. Place bacon on a microwave-safe plate and heat in microwave 1 minute to crisp. Crumble and set aside. Place spring mix in a large bowl. Arrange bacon, avocado, tomatoes and turkey on top. Drizzle with dressing and serve.

Note: For a traditional presentation, arrange the avocados, tomatoes, turkey and bacon in rows on top of the greens.

Nutritional Information (per serving):
Calories: 540 Total Fat: 45g Saturated Fat: 11g Cholesterol: 65mg Carbohydrate: 18g Sugar: 7g Fiber: 6g Protein: 22g Sodium: 1420mg Vitamin A: 45% Vitamin C: 35% Calcium: 20% Iron:10%

Serves 6

tuscan tuna

Tuna salad doesn't have to be rich to be delicious. This lightened version showcases white beans and crispy vegetables for the perfect combination of creamy and crunchy.

2 stalks celery
½ red onion, quartered
½ cup parsley
6 oz./170 g can white tuna, drained
15 oz./425 g can white beans, drained and rinsed
¾ cup Red Wine Vinaigrette (see pg 67)
salt and pepper

Add celery, onion and parsley to the base of the **Chop 'N Prep™ Chef.** Pull cord 5-6 times to finely chop. Combine celery mixture and remaining ingredients together in a large bowl. Add salt and pepper to taste. Serve immediately, or refrigerate for up to three days.

Nutritional Information (per serving):
Calories: 250 Total Fat: 19g Saturated Fat: 2.5g Cholesterol: 10mg Carbohydrate: 12g Sugar: 2g Fiber: 3g Protein: 11g Sodium: 230mg Vitamin A: 10% Vitamin C: 15% Calcium: 4% Iron: 8%

Your little ones will love the delicious, fun salads included in this section. Designed with kids in mind, they're full of things they already love. They'll never know that these dishes are also packed with healthy fruits and vegetables to keep them growing strong. These are salads sure to leave them with happy tummies and smiling faces.

salads for healthy, happy kids

Serves 6

ballgame

Your little slugger will love this fun way to eat every kids baseball game favorite—hot dogs! For a lower-fat option, choose turkey hot dogs instead.

¼ cup ketchup
¼ cup low-fat mayonnaise
¼ cup sweet pickled relish
1 tbsp. whole-grain mustard
1 tsp. vegetable oil
6 hot dogs, cut into 1-inch slices
8 oz./225 g bagged coleslaw mix
10 oz./285 g bagged mixed lettuce
4 small vine-ripe tomatoes, diced
½ cup gherkin pickles, diced
salt and pepper

In base of the **Whip 'N Prep™ Chef**, place ketchup, mayonnaise, relish and mustard. Replace cover and turn handle to thoroughly mix. Set aside or refrigerate, if not using immediately.

Heat vegetable oil in a **Chef Series™ 11"/ 28 cm Fry Pan** over medium-high heat. Add the hot dog pieces and cook for 5 minutes or until hot dogs are heated through.

In a serving bowl, toss lettuce, coleslaw mix, tomatoes, pickles and prepared dressing together. Top with hot dog pieces. Serve immediately.

Nutritional Information (per serving):
Calories: 240 Total Fat: 18g Saturated Fat: 6g Cholesterol: 30mg Carbohydrate: 15g Sugar: 10g Fiber: 2g Protein: 16g Sodium: 890mg Vitamin A: 30% Vitamin C: 40% Calcium: 4% Iron: 6%

Serves 8

creamy macaroni & ranch

A lighter, well-balanced alternative to mac 'n cheese, this pasta salad incorporates homemade ranch dressing and fun pasta shapes kids will love.

8 oz./225 g uncooked wagon wheels pasta, or any small pasta
1 lb./455 g bag frozen mixed vegetables
1 small red pepper, quartered
2 cups chicken (cooked in the **Tupperware® SmartSteamer** or rotisserie), diced
Light Ranch Dressing (see page 63)
salt and pepper

Place frozen vegetables in Steamer Base of **Tupperware® SmartSteamer**. Microwave on high for 10 minutes. Remove Steamer Base and rinse vegetables under cold water to stop cooking. Bring 2 Qts/1.8 L salted water to a boil in a **Chef Series™ 3-Qt. / 2.8 L Saucepan**. Add pasta and cook 9 minutes or until *al dente*. Drain pasta and rinse with cold water until completely cool. Place red pepper in base of **Chop 'N Prep™ Chef**. Replace cover and pull cord 2–3 times to coarsely chop. Place pasta, chicken, vegetables and red pepper in a large bowl. Toss with dressing, salt and pepper to taste.

Nutritional Information (per serving):
Calories: 260 Total Fat: 6g Saturated Fat: 2g Cholesterol: 40mg Carbohydrate: 32g Sugar: 5g
Fiber: 2g Protein: 17g Sodium: 120mg Vitamin A: 30% Vitamin C: 30% Calcium: 6% Iron: 8%

Serves 6

lit'l nuggets

Instead of fries, serve your little ones chicken nuggets on top of a fun confetti salad of shredded lettuce and cheddar cheese. A light and tangy dressing makes this a sure-fire hit.

½ cup light mayonnaise
2 tbsp. honey
2 tbsp. yellow mustard
2 tbsp. lemon juice
8 oz./225 g bagged taco-style shredded lettuce
8 oz./225 g bagged slaw mix
1 cup mini hard pretzels
1 cup shredded cheddar cheese
1 cup grape tomatoes, halved
6 breaded prepared chicken fingers, cut into chunks
salt and pepper

In base of **Whip 'N Prep™ Chef**, place mayonnaise, honey, mustard and lemon juice. Replace cover and turn handle to thoroughly mix. Set aside or refrigerate if not using immediately. In a large bowl, combine lettuce, slaw mix and prepared dressing. Top with pretzels, cheese, tomatoes and chicken. Serve immediately.

Note: Chicken fingers can be purchased in the deli section or with convenience foods in the refrigerated or freezer section of your store.

Nutritional Information (per serving):
Calories: 350 Total Fat: 20g Saturated Fat: 6g Cholesterol: 50mg Carbohydrate: 26g Sugar: 10g Fiber: 3g Protein: 18g Sodium: 770mg Vitamin A: 15% Vitamin C: 40% Calcium: 15% Iron: 6%

Serves 4

orange you delicious!

This is a sweet-tart treat for the whole family. With lots of vitamins A & C, this salad will help your kids develop good vision and healthy bones.

10 oz./285 g bagged matchstick carrots
or
10 oz./285 g carrots, grated with
Grate 'N Measure™ Grater
1 cup dried cranberries
1 tbsp. poppy seeds
8 oz./225 g can pineapple tidbits and juice
½ cup orange juice
salt and pepper

Place matchstick or grated carrots in base of **Quick Chef** and and turn handle to quickly chop into smaller pieces. Combine all ingredients in a serving bowl. Refrigerate several hours for flavors to develop. Serve cold.

Nutritional Information (per serving):
Calories: 180 Total Fat: 1.5g Saturated Fat: 0g Cholesterol: 0mg Carbohydrate: 43g Sugar: 32g Fiber: 5g Protein: 1g Sodium: 55mg Vitamin A: 240% Vitamin C: 45% Calcium: 6% Iron: 4%

Fresh salad dressing is easy, preservative-free and fun to make. Whether it's creamy ranch or zesty vinaigrette, making your own dressings at home will save money and add fresh flavor to your salad creations. These dressings vary in flavor and cultural inspiration. Use your imagination to mix and match dressings and salads for a different flavor profile every time.

salad dressings

basil vinaigrette

Makes ½ cup

½ cup fresh basil leaves
2 tbsp. balsamic vinegar
1 tbsp. honey
½ cup olive oil
salt and pepper

Add fresh basil leaves to base of **Chop 'N Prep™ Chef**. Pull cord 4–5 times to chop. Add basil, balsamic vinegar, honey, olive oil, salt and pepper to a **Quick Shake® Container**. Replace cover and shake until well incorporated.

Nutritional Information (per serving):
Calories: 280 Total Fat: 28g Saturated Fat: 4g
Cholesterol: 0mg Carbohydrate: 6g Sugar: 6g
Fiber: 0g Protein: 0g Sodium: 0mg

cilantro-lime vinaigrette

Makes 2 cups

1 cup vegetable stock
1½ tsp. arrowroot powder or cornstarch
½ cup fresh lime juice
½ tsp. sugar
2 tbsp. sesame oil
¼ cup peanut oil
2 tbsp. canola oil
2 tbsp. sea salt
1 tsp. cilantro

Combine arrowroot with 1½ tsp. cold stock and mix to form a paste. Bring the remaining stock to a boil in a small saucepan and stir in arrowroot paste. Boil until thickened, about 2 minutes. Remove from heat and cool. Add lime juice and sugar and stir to combine. Cool completely in the refrigerator or in a bowl set over ice. Place cooled mixture in a **Quick Shake® Container**. Add oil, replace seal and shake well to mix. Add salt and cilantro.

Nutritional Information (per serving):
Calories: 70 Total Fat: 7g Saturated Fat: 1g
Cholesterol: 0mg Carbohydrate: 1g Sugar: 1g
Fiber: 0g Protein: 0g Sodium: 710mg

greek

Makes ½ cup

4 tbsp. lemon juice
2 garlic cloves, chopped
¼ cup extra virgin olive oil

Add all ingredients to a **Quick Shake® Container**. Replace cover and shake until well combined.

Nutritional Information (per serving):
Calories: 130 Total Fat: 14g Saturated Fat: 2g
Cholesterol: 0mg Carbohydrate: 2mg Sugar: 0mg
Fiber: 0g Protein: 0g Sodium: 0mg

honey mustard

Makes ¾ cup

½ cup light mayonnaise
2 tbsp. honey
2 tbsp. yellow mustard
2 tbsp. lemon juice
salt and pepper

In base of **Whip 'N Prep™ Chef**, place mayonnaise, honey, mustard, lemon juice and seasonings. Replace cover and turn handle to thoroughly mix.

Nutritional Information (per serving):
Calories: 80 Total Fat: 6g Saturated Fat: 1g
Cholesterol: 5mg Carbohydrate: 7g Sugar: 6g
Fiber: 0g Protein: 0g Sodium: 160mg

light ranch

Makes ¾ cup

½ cup buttermilk
½ cup light sour cream
¼ cup light mayonnaise
1 tbsp. lemon juice
1 tbsp. chives
1 clove garlic
salt and pepper

Place garlic and chives in bowl of **Chop 'N Prep™ Chef**. Replace cover and pull cord 4–5 times to finely chop. Place buttermilk, sour cream, mayonnaise in base of **Whip 'N Prep™ Chef**. With **Tupperware® Lemon Lime Press**, squeeze lemon juice into container, add garlic and chives. Replace cover, turn handle to blend thoroughly.

Nutritional Information (per serving):
Calories: 35 Total Fat: 3g Saturated Fat: 1g
Cholesterol: 5mg Carbohydrate: 2g Sugar: 1g
Fiber: 0g Protein: 1g Sodium: 40mg

peanut
Makes 1 1/8 cup

¼ cup, plus 1 tbsp. all-natural
or fresh-ground peanut butter
2 tbsp. honey
1 tsp. soy sauce
¼ cup rice vinegar
¼ cup canola oil
1 tbsp. sesame oil
2 tbsp. warm water
salt and pepper

Combine all ingredients in base of **Whip 'N Prep™ Chef**. Replace with cover and blend together until mixture is smooth. Keep refrigerated for up to 1 week.

Nutritional Information (per serving):
Calories: 130 Total Fat: 12g Saturated Fat: 1.5g
Cholesterol: 0mg Carbohydrate: 6g Sugar: 5g
Fiber: 1g Protein: 2g Sodium: 80mg

pesto vinaigrette
Makes ¾ cup

2/3 cup prepared pesto sauce
2 tbsp. white wine vinegar
3 tbsp. extra virgin olive oil
salt and pepper

Place pesto, vinegar, salt and pepper in a **Quick Shake® Container**. Add olive oil, replace seal and shake until ingredients are well incorporated.

Nutritional Information (per serving):
Calories: 210 Total Fat: 22g Saturated Fat: 3.5g
Cholesterol: 0mg Carbohydrate: 1g Sugar: 0g
Fiber: 0g Protein: 2g Sodium: 40mg

pesto sauce
Makes 2/3 cup

¾ cup packed basil leaves
3 tbsp. pine nuts, toasted
1 clove garlic
¼ cup grated Parmesan cheese
½ cup extra virgin olive oil
salt and pepper

Place basil, pine nuts, garlic, Parmesan cheese and oil in base of **Chop 'N Prep™ Chef**. Replace cover, twist to seal and pull cord 4–5 times until finely chopped. Season with salt and pepper.

Nutritional Information (per serving):
Calories: 160 Total Fat: 17g Saturated Fat: 2.5g
Cholesterol: 0mg Carbohydrate: 1g Sugar: 0g
Fiber: 0g Protein: 2g Sodium: 40mg

poppy seed
Makes ¾ cup

½ cup mayonnaise
2 tbsp. honey
½ tbsp. Dijon mustard
1 tbsp. apple cider vinegar
2 tbsp. lemon juice
½ tbsp. poppy seeds
salt and pepper

Add all ingredients to base of **Quick Shake® Container**. Replace cover and shake until well combined.

Nutritional Information (per serving):
Calories: 90 Total Fat: 7g Saturated Fat: 1g
Cholesterol: 5mg Carbohydrate: 8g Sugar: 7g
Fiber: 0g Protein: 0g Sodium: 260mg

raspberry red wine vinaigrette
Makes 1 cup

¼ cup raspberry red wine vinegar
¾ cup olive oil
1 tsp. Dijon mustard
2 cloves garlic, minced
salt and pepper

Add all ingredients to **Quick Shake® Container**. Replace seal and shake until well combined.

Nutritional Information (per serving):
Calories: 190 Total Fat: 21g Saturated Fat: 3g
Cholesterol: 0mg Carbohydrate: 0g Sugar: 0g
Fiber: 0g Protein: 0g Sodium: 15mg

red wine vinaigrette

Makes ¾ cup

¼ cup red wine vinegar
2 tbsp. lemon juice
1 tsp. honey
½ cup extra virgin olive oil
salt and pepper

Add all ingredients to **Quick Shake® Container.** Replace seal and shake until well combined.

Nutritional Information (per serving):
Calories: 170 Total Fat: 19g Saturated Fat: 2.5g
Cholesterol: 0mg Carbohydrate: 1g Sugar: 1g
Fiber: 0g Protein: 0g Sodium: 0mg

sizzlin' vinaigrette

Makes 1 1/8 cup

½ tsp. cayenne pepper
¼ cup white wine vinegar
1 tsp. salt
1 tsp. dry mustard
2½ tsp. sugar
1 tsp. garlic powder
10–12 drops hot pepper sauce
¾ cup vegetable oil

Combine all ingredients, except for vegetable oil, in **Quick Shake® Container.** Shake until combined. Remove the flip-top seal, add the vegetable oil, replace seal and shake until well incorporated.

Nutritional Information (per serving):
Calories: 170 Total Fat: 18g Saturated Fat: 1.5g
Cholesterol: 0mg Carbohydrate: 2g Sugar: 1g
Fiber: 0g Protein: 0g Sodium: 270mg

sweet & sour

Makes 1 cup

½ cup canola oil
½ cup sugar
¼ cup apple cider vinegar
salt and pepper

Place all ingredients in **Quick Shake® Container**. Replace seal and shake until well combined.

Nutritional Information (per serving):
Calories: 140 Total Fat: 11g Saturated Fat: 1g
Cholesterol: 0mg Carbohydrate: 10g Sugar: 10g
Fiber: 0g Protein: 0g Sodium: 60mg

thai

Makes 1/3 cup

½ jalapeño pepper, seeded
¼ cup lime juice
1 tbsp. Thai fish sauce
2 tsp. sesame oil
½ tsp. sugar

Chop jalapeño finely with the **Chef Series™ Pro Utility Knife.** Add jalapeño, lime, fish sauce, sesame oil and sugar to **Quick Shake® Container.** Replace cover and shake until well combined.

Nutritional Information (per serving):
Calories: 30 Total Fat: 2.5g Saturated Fat: 0g
Cholesterol: 0mg Carbohydrate: 2g Sugar: 1g
Fiber: 0g Protein: 0g Sodium: 350mg

ensaladas sensacionales

para ti y tu familia

"¿Qué fue el paraíso sino un jardín repleto de hortalizas, hierbas y gustos? Nada más que delicias".

- William Lawson

contenido

Es fácil elogiar un jugoso bistec o un delicioso postre, pero es un verdadero éxito cuando preparamos una ensalada memorable. Vegetales maduros, lechuga crujiente, ingredientes coloridos y aderezos sabrosos tienen que combinar con éxito para lograr un plato sensacional. Sea acompañando a un plato principal o la alternativa para una comida pesada, las ensaladas son la manera que usan los cocineros con imaginación para expresarse.

El recipiente **Saludable para Ensaladera Portátil** de Tupperware es la manera perfecta de llevar la frescura adonde te lleve el día. Tres opciones separadas hacen de este producto el medio ideal para transportar ensaladas, siempre listo cuando tú lo necesitas.

El recipiente incluye sello virtualmente hermético para que no te preocupes por derrames ni deterioro. El sello incorpora un cuchillo y tenedor que encajan juntos y un recipiente Midgets®, que se acomoda perfectamente con tus aliños preparados en casa para usar luego con tu ensalada. Cuando vayas a comer, vierte el aliño sobre los vegetales frescos para obtener una saludable y refrescante opción para el almuerzo.

Este libro de recetas incluye 24 ensaladas y 13 aliños para que los combines. Usando como inspiración desde la comida tailandesa a ensaladas de pasta, estas creaciones llenas de frescura fueron diseñadas contigo y tu familia en mente. **¡Buen provecho!**

Espinaca Tierna
Se le considera la opción más saludable y su color verde oscuro, y sabor suave, la convierten en una delicia.

Arúgula
La arúgula de hoja larga tiene un sabor característico picante, con ciertos toques de hierbas y especias. Es un vegetal que combina bien en ensaladas dulces con frutas.

Romana
Famosa por ser la estrella de la clásica ensalada césar, la lechuga romana presenta hojas verde claro en su interior y hojas exteriores verde oscuro. Su sabor es fresco y su consistencia, crujiente.

Lechuga Bibb
Suave y cremosa, esta lechuga es la alternativa a la lechuga clásica iceberg de sabor ligeramente dulce.

Mezcla de Vegetales
Si prefieres una mezcla de vegetales en bolsa, ésta es la mejor opción. Una combinación de sabores, colores y texturas que añaden atractivo y sabor al paladar.

virtuosas verduras

Las verduras son mucho más que una simple lechuga iceberg. Prueba las nuevas hortalizas, como arúgula picante o una cremosa lechuga Bibb, la próxima vez que uses tu Recipiente Saludable de Ensaladera Portátil.

Lechuga de Hoja Roja

De dramático color marrón, la lechuga de hoja roja añade su distintivo color a cualquier plato. Se caracteriza por su sabor suave, similar al de la lechuga verde.

Lechuga de Hoja Verde

Sus hojas crespas y su sabor casi dulce la convierten en la favorita de los fanáticos de las ensaladas. Una excelente alternativa de la lechuga romana o iceberg, por su sabor neutral.

Radicchio

De color rojo vino, el radicchio es ideal para cocinar a la parrilla realzando algo de su dulzura. Combinado con otros vegetales, el radicchio ofrece un claro contraste.

Lechuga *Iceberg*

Esta lechuga clásica es crujiente y refrescante. Se mantiene bien en el refrigerador, por semanas, si la almacenas correctamente.

Col Tipo Napa

Hojas, largas, anchas y rizadas de sabor suave caracterizan a este miembro de la familia de las coles chinas.

Lechuga Crespa

(ver página 78)

Este tipo de lechuga francesa tiene elegantes hojas rizadas, un ligero sabor amargo y combina muy bien con ingredientes cremosos como yema de huevo o un aliño cremoso.

espectaculares ensaladas para acompañar

No te conformes con guarniciones simples usando un sólo ingrediente. Estas ensaladas pueden ser las estrellas de la velada. Una buena ensalada añade interés visual y complejidad de sabores a la cena. Servir una comida que todos recuerden es tan fácil como combinar ingredientes frescos, sabores originales y buena nutrición. Guarda el brócoli al vapor por una noche y prepara una ensalada fácil y sabrosa.

Rinde 4 porciones

Una deliciosa alternativa al arroz blanco. Esta ensalada incorpora aceitunas saladas kalamata, maíz y cebollines, resultando en un impresionante color y sabor.

arroz basmati

- 1 taza de arroz Basmati
- 2 tazas de agua
- ⅓ taza de aceite canola
- 3 Cucharadas de vinagre de vino blanco
- 1 cucharadita de mostaza Dijon
- 1 cucharadita de miel
- ¼ cucharadita de jengibre en polvo
- 1 taza de maiz fresco o congelado, cocido
- 2 cebollines, picados
- ½ taza de anacardos, picados
- 1 taza de aceitunas Kalamata sin semilla, picadas
- sal y pimienta

Combina el arroz con 2 tazas de agua en la **Arrocera Tupperware® para Microondas**. Tapa y cocina al microondas, en Potencia Alta, por 5 minutos. Luego cocina al microondas en potencia Mediana por 15 minutos. Deja reposar 5 minutos. Esponja con una cuchara para servir y reserva.

Para preparar el aliño, combina el aceite, vinagre, mostaza, miel y jengibre en el **Recipiente Quick Shake®**. Sazona con sal y pimienta. Reserva.

Para preparar la ensalada, combina el arroz cocido, aliño e ingredientes restantes en un tazón grande. Revuelve y sirve tibio, a temperatura del ambiente o fría.

Información Nutricional (por porción): Calorías: 250 Grasa Total: 15g Grasa Saturada: 1.5g Colesterol: 0mg Carbohidratos: 28g Azúcar: 1g Fibra: 2g Proteína: 4g Sodio: 190mg Vitamina A: 3% Vitamina C: 5% Calcio: 3% Hierro: 7%

Rinde 4 porciones

Sirve esta ensalada ligera en el verano, cuando los tomates y albahaca están en su mayor frescura.

caprese

- 8 oz/225g de mozzarella fresca, en agua
- 6 tomates pequeños, madurados en la rama
- Vinagreta de Albahaca (ver página 89)
- ½ taza de hojitas de albahaca fresca
- sal y pimienta

Con el **Cuchillo Chef Series™ Pro Multiusos Serrado**, rebana los tomates y la mozzarella fresca en círculos. Coloca las tajadas de tomate, albahaca fresca y mozzarella, una sobre otra, para servir. Rocía con Vinagreta de Albahaca y sazona con sal y pimienta al gusto.

Nota: La Ensalada Caprese que sobre puede ser añadida a una pasta o mezclada con verduras para crear una ensalada.

Información Nutricional (por porción): Calorías: 470 Grasa Total: 41g Grasa Saturada: 11g Colesterol: 45mg Carbohidratos: 13g Azúcar: 10g Fibra: 2g Proteína: 14g Sodio: 360mg Vitamina A: 40% Vitamina C: 30% Calcio: 30% Hierro: 6%

Rinde 6 porciones

Este ceviche estilo mexicano es delicioso para una barbacoa o un picnic, complementando las carnes a la parrilla con algo ligero.

ceviche veracruz

1 libra/455g de langostinos, pelados y sin vena (retira las colas)
jugo de 2 limones
jugo de 2 limas
jugo de 2 naranjas
1 pepino, pelado y sin semillas
½ taza de cebolla roja, pelada y picada
2 pimientos jalapeños, sin semillas
1 tomate, sin semillas
1 aguacate, sin semilla
¼ taza de cilantro
sal y pimienta

Revuelve los langostinos con la mitad de los jugos cítricos y coloca en la **Vaporera Inteligente Tupperware®**. Llena la Bandeja para Agua con 1¾ tazas de agua. Cocina al microondas, en Potencia Alta, por 7 minutos. Retira del microondas, coloca los langostinos en el **Quick Chef**, colocándole la hoja y pica grueso. Transfiere a un tazón grande. Añade el jugo restante al tazón. Reserva.

Coloca el pepino, cebolla y jalapeño en la base del **Quick Chef** y pica grueso. Transfiere al tazón con los langostinos. Coloca el tomate, aguacate y cilantro en la base del **Quick Chef** y gira la manija, picando grueso. Añade al tazón. Revuelve los ingredientes y sazona al gusto. Sirve con hojuelas de tortilla si gustas.

Información Nutricional (por porción): Calorías: 150 Grasa Total: 6g Grasa Saturada: 1g Colesterol: 110mg Carbohidratos: 11g Azúcar: 5g Fibra: 3g Proteína: 14g Sodio: 135mg Vitamina A: 10% Vitamina C: 60% Calcio: 4% Hierro: 10%

Rinde 4 porciones

La perfecta combinación de ingredientes frescos y de gran calidad han hecho que esta ensalada sea una de las favoritas por años. Las Tostadas de Pan Pita son ideales para levantar hasta el último trozo de queso feta.

griega con tostadas de pan pita

4 pedazos de pan pita, cortados en cuatro
½ cucharadita de orégano seco
1 cucharadita de aceite de oliva extra virgen
10 oz/285g de ensalada *romaine*
1 pepino
1 tomate
1 taza de aceitunas negras
2 cebollines
½ taza de Aderezo Griego (ver página 89)
¾ taza de queso Feta desmenuzado

Calentar el horno a 350°F/175°C.

Coloca el pan pita en una lámina para hornear. Rocía el pan con aceite de oliva. Salpica con orégano seco, sal y pimienta. Hornea por 10 minutos o hasta que el pan pita esté crujiente.

Mientras el pan pita está tostándose, prepara la ensalada. Coloca el pepino, tomate, aceitunas negras y cebollines en la base del **Quick Chef**. Gira el asa, picando grueso. Combina la ensalada con el pepino, tomate, aceitunas y cebollines. Revuelve los vegetales con ¼ taza de aderezo. Adorna con el queso y pan pita caliente. Sirve de inmediato.

Información Nutricional (por porción): Calorías: 280 Grasa Total: 16g Grasa Saturada: 4g Colesterol: 10mg Carbohidratos: 27g Azúcar: 3g Fibra: 6g Proteína: 10g Sodio: 830mg Vitamina A: 140% Vitamina C: 45% Calcio: 15% Hierro: 15%

Rinde 6 porciones

Esta popular ensalada se sirve en la mayoría de bistros en París. El intenso sabor del queso de cabra y huevo escalfado complementa la lechuga crespa.

bistro de parís

- 1 hogaza de pan baguette (pan francés), cortado en 20 tajadas
- 5 oz/140g de queso de cabra
- 1 lechuga crespa
- ½ taza de nueces picadas
- pimienta negra
- 6 huevo, escalfado o frito
- Vinagreta Picante (ver pág. 00)

Calienta el horno en la función "broiler". Rebana el pan baguette con el **Cuchillo Chef Series™ Pro para Pan.** Usa el **Cuchillo Chef Series™ Pro de Precisión** para rebanar el queso en tajadas finas. Coloca una tajada de queso sobre cada trozo de pan para preparar un crutón. Rocía con pimienta negra si deseas. Coloca al horno hasta que el queso se dore. Acomoda las hojas de lechuga crespa en los platos para ensalada, coloca el huevo, adorna con 2 ó 3 crutones y rocía con nueces.

Información Nutricional (por porción): Calorías: 590 Grasa Total:40g Grasa Saturada: 6g Colesterol: 45mg Carbohidratos: 45g Azúcar: 3g Fibra: 5g Proteína: 16g Sodio: 950mg Vitamina A: 45% Vitamina C: 10% Calcio: 10% Hierro: 20%

Rinde 5 porciones

La quinoa es un grano y una buena fuente de proteína y aminoácidos que puede ayudar con el funcionamiento del sistema inmunológico y salud en general. La suave fragancia de la naranja añade elegancia a esta ensalada.

quinoa con aroma a naranja y frijoles negros

- 1 taza de quinoa
- 1½ tazas de caldo de pollo sin grasa
- ½ taza de jugo de naranja fresco
- 1 Cucharada de ralladura de naranja
- ⅓ taza de aceite de oliva extra virgen
- 2 dientes de ajo, molidos
- jugo de 1 lima
- ¼ taza de cilantro, picado
- 1 Cucharada de mostaza Dijon
- 1 Cucharada de Mezcla Simple Indulgence™ Chipotle del Sudoeste
- 1 pimiento amarillo pequeño, cortado en cuatro pedazos
- 2 tomates medianos madurados en rama, picados
- 1 lata de 15 oz/425g de frijoles negros, escurridos
- 1 pimiento rojo pequeño, sin semillas y cortado en trozos grandes
- sal y pimienta

Combina la quinoa, caldo de pollo, jugo y ralladura de naranja en la **Arrocera Tupperware® para Microondas**. Tapa y cocina en el microondas, en Potencia Alta, de 15 a 18 minutos. Esponja con una cuchara para serivr. Coloca el aceite de oliva, ajo, jugo de lima, cilantro, mostaza Dijon y Mezcla de Condimentos en el **Recipiente Quick Shake®**. Coloca el sello y sacude bien. Acomoda los pimientos rojo y amarillo en la base del **Chef Picador Chop 'N Prep™**, vuelve a sellar y hala el cordón, de 2 a 3 veces, picando grueso. Coloca los pimientos e ingredientes restantes con la quinoa cocida en un tazón familiar. Revuelve los vegetales y quinoa cocida con el aliño. Sazona con sal y pimienta al gusto.

Información Nutricional (por porción): Calorías: 340 Grasa Total: 17g Grasa Saturada: 2.5g Colesterol: 30mg Carbohidratos: 40g Azúcar: 7g Fibra: 6g Proteína: 10g Sodio: 610mg Vitamina A: 2% Vitamina C: 40% Calcio: 4% Hierro: 15%

Rinde 4 porciones

Si te gustan los quesos Roquefort, elige los de buena calidad. "Maytag y Danish blues" son algunos de los mejores y rinden más.

espinaca y pera

- 1 paquete de hojas de espinaca tierna
- 2 peras Anjou, peladas, sin corazón y en tajadas
- ½ taza de nueces partidas por la mitad
- ½ taza de queso Gorgonzola o Roquefort desmenuzado
- Aliño de Semilla de Amapola (ver página 90)

Coloca la espinaca y peras en un tazón grande. Coloca las nueces en la base del Quick Chef. Reemplaza la cubierta y gira el asa para picar grueso. Añade a la espinaca y tajadas de pera. Rocía el queso sobre la ensalada y el aliño. Revuelve para combinar

Información Nutricional (por porción): Calorías: 340 Grasa Total: 23g Grasa Saturada: 5g Colesterol: 25mg Carbohidratos: 31g Azúcar: 19g Fibra: 6g Proteína: 8g Sodio: 630mg Vitamina A: 120% Vitamina C: 40% Calcio: 20% Hierro: 15%

Rinde 4 porciones

Las fresas están en su mejor época de marzo a agosto, de manera que esta ensalada será una delicia durante las noches de verano. Convierte esta ensalada en algo especial, añadiendo trozos de pollo asado, tofu o bistec.

espinaca y fresas

- ½ libra de fresas en rebanadas
- 10 oz/285g de espinaca tierna
- 4 oz/115g queso de cabra desmenuzado
- 2 Cucharadas de piñones, tostados
- Aliño de Mostaza con Miel (ver página 89)

En un tazón mediano, combina las fresas y la espinaca tierna. Rocía con queso de cabra desmenuzado y los piñones tostados. Rocía con tu aliño favorito.

Nota: Esta ensalada puede convertirse en un plato principal añadiendo pechuga de pollo a la parrilla o al vapor, langostinos, salmón o carne de res (falda o vacío) a la parrilla.

Información Nutricional (por porción): Calorías: 190 Grasa Total: 13g Grasa Saturada: 7g Colesterol: 30mg Carbohidratos: 8g Azúcar: 4g Fibra: 3g Proteína: 12g Sodio: 150mg Vitamina A: 130% Vitamina C: 90% Calcio: 35% Hierro:15%

Rinde 8 porciones

Una pequeña cucharada de crema de leche batida, preparada en casa, realza el sabor de esta versión isleña de ensalada de fruta. Las almendras y el coco desmenuzado añaden sabor y consistencia.

frutas veraniegas

- 2 tazas de melón
- 2 tazas de sandía
- 1 libra/455g de fresas, retira los tallos
- 2 kiwis, pelados
- 1 taza de crema concentrada/ heavy de leche
- 2 Cucharadas de azúcar superfina
- 1 cucharadita de extracto de ron, opcional
- ½ taza de coco rallado, tostado
- ½ taza de almendras en rebanadas, tostadas

Con el **Cuchillo Chef Series™ Pro del Chef**, corta la fruta y colócala en un tazón mediano. Coloca la crema de leche concentrada en la base de la **Batidora Whip 'N Prep™**; sella y gira la manija para batir hasta que la crema empiece a espesar. Añade el azúcar y extracto, y bate hasta formar picos. Rocía con coco y almendras; cubre la ensalada de frutas con la crema batida. Sirve de inmediato.

Información Nutricional (por porción): Calorías: 240 Grasa Total: 16g Grasa Saturada: 9g Colesterol: 40mg Carbohidratos: 23g Azúcar: 16g Fibra: 4g Proteína: 4g Sodio: 20mg Vitamina A: 45% Vitamina C: 170% Calcio: 6% Hierro: 6%

Rinde 6 porciones

Inspirada en un viaje a Hawai, esta ensalada mezcla sabores del mar y tierra con sabores tropicales, resultando en una fabulosa experiencia.

playera de langostinos

- 1 libra/455 g de langostinos cocidos, pelados y sin vena
- 1 piña, pelada, sin corazón y cortada en trozos
- 2 mangos, pelados y cortados en trozos
- 2 bananas, en tajadas
- 1 Cucharada de coco rallado, tostado
- 1 Cucharada de anacardos, tostados y picados
- 2 Cucharadas de aceite canola
- 2 Cucharadas de café pasado
- 1 Cucharada de salsa de soja, baja de sodio
- 1 limón, jugo y ralladura
- 2 Cucharadas de leche de coco ligera
- 1 pimiento habanero, sin semillas
- ½ taza de cilantro, picado
- 1 cucharadita de jengibre fresco, molido
- sal y pimienta al gusto

6 tazas de arúgula, opcional

Coloca los langostinos, piña, mango, bananas, coco y anacardos en un tazón grande. Revuelve para combinar. Añade el aceite, café, salsa de soja, jugo de limón y leche de coco a la base del **Recipiente Quick Shake®** y reserva. Coloca el pimiento habanero, cilantro y jengibre en el **Chef Picador Chop 'N Prep™** y hala el cordón, de 4 a 5 veces, o hasta que el contenido esté finamente picado. Añade la mezcla al **Recipiente Quick Shake®**, coloca la cubierta y sacude bien. Vierte el aliño sobre los langostinos con la fruta y refrigera como mínimo 1 hora. Sirve sobre arugula, si deseas.

Información Nutricional (por porción): Calorías: 290 Grasa Total: 7g Grasa Saturada: 1g Colesterol: 145mg Carbohidratos: 43g Azúcar: 30g Fibra: 5g Proteína: 18g Sodio: 240mg Vitamina A: 20% Vitamina C: 180% Calcio: 6% Hierro: 20%

ensaladas como plato principal

Las ensaladas también pueden hacerte sentir completamente satisfecha. Prueba una de estas maravillas como plato principal. Combina lechugas crujientes con vegetales y frutas de brillantes colores; así añades proteínas a la ensalada para quedar satisfecha sin sentir pereza. Añade frijoles, tofu, cerdo, bistec, pescado o pollo a cualquier ensalada para preparar un plato principal sensacional.

Rinde 8 porciones

Curry ahumado y mango fresco complementan el estilo de esta fantástica versión de ensalada clásica de pollo.

bombay de pollo y mango

- ⅓ taza de yogur estilo griego, simple y sin grasa
- ⅓ taza de mayonesa con poca grasa
- 1 Cucharada de curry en polvo
- 3 Cucharadas de jugo de limón
- 1 Cucharada de miel
- 3 pechugas de pollo cocidas, picadas (cocidas a fuego lento o al vapor en la **Vaporera Inteligente Tupperware®**)
- 1 mango maduro, pelado, sin semilla y picado
- 1 taza de uvas rojas sin semilla, por la mitad
- 1 lata de 8 oz/225g de castañas de agua, escurridas
- ½ taza de anacardos con sal, asados
- sal y pimienta

En tu tazón familiar favorito o en la **Batidora Whip 'N Prep™**, revuelve el yogurt, mayonesa, curry en polvo, jugo de limón y miel. Añade los ingredientes restantes y combina suavemente con el aliño. Sirve de inmediato o refrigera hasta por tres días.

Información Nutricional (por porción): Calorías: 190 Grasa Total: 8g Grasa Saturada: 1.5g Colesterol: 30mg Carbohidratos: 17g Azúcar: 11g Fibra: 2g Proteína: 13g Sodio: 120mg Vitamina A: 4% Vitamina C: 20% Calcio: 2% Hierro: 8%

Rinde 6 porciones

La lechuga crujiente complementa la cremosa consistencia de los anacardos y los auténticos sabores orientales en estas divertidas copas de lechuga fáciles de comer.

copas de lechuga con pollo y anacardos

- 1 cabeza de lechuga iceberg o Bibb
- 3 Pechugas de pollo (escalfadas o cocidas al vapor en la **Vaporera Inteligente Tupperware®** al microondas)
- 1 cucharadita de aceite de ajonjolí
- ½ cebolla amarilla, picada
- 1 trozo de 1 pulgada de jengibre fresco
- 6 dientes de ajo
- ¾ taza de salsa oriental/hoisin
- 5 Cucharadas de salsa de soja o tamari
- 1 cucharadita de salsa dulce-picante
- 1 taza de anacardos, picados

Para preparar las copas de lechuga, separa las hojas externas de la lechuga con cuidado para no romperlas. Lava, seca y acomoda en un plato de servir. Pica las pechugas en trozos pequeños. Reserva.

En la **Sartén Chef Series™ de 11"/ 28 cm con Tapa**, calienta el aceite de ajonjolí sobre fuego Mediano. Mientras calienta, pica la cebolla, el jengibre y ajo en el **Quick Chef**. Añade la mezcla a la sartén y cocina 5 minutos hasta que los vegetales estén suaves. Añade el pollo, anacardos, las salsas *hoisin*, de soja y salsa dulce-picante. Revuelve y cocina hasta calentar. Sirve de inmediato con las copas de lechuga para que cada quien prepare su copa a su gusto.

Información Nutricional (por porción): Calorías: 300 Grasa Total: 14g Grasa Saturada: 2.5g Colesterol: 40g Carbohidratos: 27g Azúcar: 13g Fibra: 3g Proteína: 20g Sodio: 1490mg Vitamina A: 10% Vitamina C: 8% Calcio: 6% Hierro: 15%

Rinde 8 porciones

La gran diferencia de esta ensalada la logra el pesto fresco que añade color a la ensalada. Las nueces añaden consistencia. Prepara el pesto un día con anticipación para que los sabores armonicen.

espinaca tierna y orzo

- Pesto (ver página 90)
- Vinagreta de Pesto (ver página 90)
- 2 tazas de pasta orzo cruda
- 2 tazas de pollo a la brasa (preparado en la **Vaporera Inteligente Tupperware®** o a la brasa)
- 8 oz/225g de tomates cerezo
- 6 oz/170g de espinaca tierna, lavada
- 2 a 3 Cucharadas de queso parmesano rallado
- sal y pimienta

Haz hervir 2 Cuartos/1.8 L de agua con sal en la **Olla Chef Series™ de 3 Cuartos/2.8 L**. Añade la pasta orzo y cocina 9 minutos o hasta que esté *al dente*. Escurre la pasta, mezcla con la espinaca, pollo, tomates y Vinagreta de Pesto. Añade queso parmesano y sal y pimienta al gusto.

Información Nutricional (por porción): Calorías: 430 Grasa Total: 24g Grasa Saturada: 4g Colesterol: 35mg Carbohidratos: 34g Azúcar: 3g Fibra: 2g Proteína: 19g Sodio: 105mg Vitamina A: 50% Vitamina C: 15% Calcio: 8% Hierro: 15%

Rinde 4 porciones

La quinoa es un grano del Perú con una textura similar al *couscous*. Está a la venta en la mayoría de supermercados y es una manera deliciosa de añadir granos integrales a tu dieta.

quinoa y lomo de cerdo

- 2 lb./1 kg de lomo de cerdo
- 1 paquete de 5.6 oz/160g de quinoa cruda
- ½ taza de corazones de alcachofa, marinados y en tajadas
- ¼ taza de aceitunas en tajadas
- ½ ramo de espinaca tierna, fresca
- 1 taza de tomates cerezo, cortados por la mitad
- 2 Cucharadas de perejil de hoja plana, finamente picado
- ¼ taza de vinagre balsámico
- 1½ Cucharadas de aceite de oliva extra virgen
- 4 dientes de ajo, molidos
- sal y pimienta

Vierte agua en la Bandeja para Agua de la **Vaporera Inteligente Tupperware®**. Coloca el lomo de cerdo en la base y ponlo en el microondas, en Alta Potencia, por 17 minutos o hasta que éste alcance una temperatura interna de 165° F/74° C. Deja reposar por 5 minutos y corta en pedazos finos.

Prepara la quinoa en la **Arrocera Tupperware® para Microondas** según las indicaciones en el inserto del producto. Deja enfriar y con una cuchara de madera, afloja la quinoa. Añade los corazones de alcachofa, aceitunas, espinaca, tomates cerezo y perejil. En un tazón pequeño, mezcla el vinagre balsámico, aceite de oliva y ajo mezclando bien; sazona con sal y pimienta al gusto y vierte sobre la ensalada. Revuelve para combinar.

Información Nutricional (por porción): Calorías: 620 Grasa Total: 26g Grasa Saturada: 6g Colesterol: 150mg Carbohidratos: 36g Azúcar: 7g Fibra: 5g Proteína: 57g Sodio: 290mg Vitamina A: 90% Vitamina C: 40% Calcio: 10% Hierro: 35%

Rinde 4 porciones

Una ensalada de sabroso estilo Tex-Mex que toda tu familia disfrutará.

pollo santa fe con quesadillas

- 1 bolsa de 10 oz/285g de vegetales surtidos para ensalada
- 1 lata de 15 oz/425g de frijoles negros, escurridos
- 1 taza de maíz congelado
- 2 pechugas de pollo
- 1 cucharadita de aceite vegetal
- 4 tortillas de harina de 8 pulgadas/10cm
- 1 taza de queso cheddar sharp rallado
- ½ taza de Vinagreta de Cilantro-Lima (ver página 89)
- sal y pimienta

En la **Vaporera Inteligente Tupperware®**, coloca el pollo en la Base de la Vaporera y el maíz congelado en el Colador. Llena la Bandeja para Agua con 1½ tazas/400 mL de agua. Cocina al microondas en Potencia Alta por 15 minutos o hasta que el pollo esté cocido. Cuando enfríe un poco, córtalo en rebanadas finas. Reserva.

Calienta el aceite vegetal en la **Sartén Chef Series de 8"/20 cm a fuego Mediano Alto**. Coloca ¼ de taza de queso a un lado de cada tortilla. Dobla la tortilla por la mitad y luego coloca en la sartén, cocinando en tandas. Cocina cada lado 2 minutos, hasta que el queso se derrita y el exterior de la tortilla esté dorado. Reserva y mantén tibio.

En un tazón de servir, mezcla los vegetales para ensalada, maíz, frijoles, pollo y el aliño. Coloca las quesadillas encima y sirve de inmediato.

Información Nutricional (por porción): Calorías: 540 Grasa Total: 24g Grasa Saturada: 8g Colesterol: 65mg Carbohidratos: 51g Azúcar: 4g Fibra: 8g Proteína: 30g Sodio: 1520mg Vitamina A: 60% Vitamina C: 8% Calcio: 25% Hierro: 80%

Rinde 4 porciones

Esta fácil y deliciosa ensalada es mejor que visitar tu restaurante de carnes favorito. Un plato que satisface cualquier apetito.

de bistec

- Filete de lomo de 2.4 oz/115 g
- 2 champiñones portobello grandes, en tajaditas
- 1 cucharadita de aceite vegetal
- 1 bolsa de 10 oz/265g de vegetales surtidos para ensalada
- ½ taza de Vinagreta de Vino Rojo y Frambuesa
- ½ taza de queso roquefort desmenuzado
- ½ taza de pimientos rojos asados de pomo, escurridos y en tajadas
- sal y pimienta

En la **Sartén Chef Series™ de 11"/28 cm**, calienta el aceite a fuego Mediano Alto. Sazona los filetes con sal y pimienta y coloca en la sartén caliente por 6 minutos, cada lado, hasta que los filetes estén cocidos a tu gusto. Retíralos y déjalos reposar sobre una tabla de cortar, por 5 minutos. Cocina los champiñones en aceite caliente hasta que estén tiernos y retíralos. Rebana la carne en tajadas finas. Mantén tibio.

Prepara la ensalada colocando los vegetales en un tazón familiar. Añade el aliño y encima la carne, champiñones, pimientos y queso. Sirve de inmediato.

Información Nutricional (por porción): Calorías: 410 Grasa Total: 35g Grasa Saturada: 9g Colesterol: 50mg Carbohidratos: 9g Azúcar: 4g Fibra: 3g Proteína: 17g Sodio: 410mg Vitamina A: 60% Vitamina C: 15% Calcio: 10% Hierro: 10%

Rinde 4 porciones

Esta ensalada oriental combina los sabores dulces, salados, agrios y naturales que hacen la comida oriental tan apetitosa. El salmón está repleto de grasas monoinsaturadas que ayudan a mantener la salud y bajar el colesterol.

salmón al vapor y col estilo oriental

1 libra/455g de filete de salmón
1 col de Napa de 2 libras
1 ramo de cebollines
1 paquete de fideos "ramen"
1 paquete de almendras en rebanadas o en láminas
3 Cucharadas de mantequilla
sal y pimienta
Aliño Agridulce (ver página 90)

Cocina el salmón al vapor por 10 minutos en la **Vaporera Inteligente Tupperware®** hasta que esté opaco. Rebana finamente la col, rebana los cebollines y coloca en un tazón grande. Calienta la mantequilla en la **Sartén Chef Series™ de 11"/28 cm** sobre fuego Mediano. Tritura los fideos y añádelos, junto con las almendras, a la mantequilla derretida. Cocina hasta dorar. Escurre bien y reserva. Justo antes de servir, añade los fideos y almendras sobre la col y revuelve con el aliño. Sirve encima el salmón al vapor.

Información Nutricional (por porción): Calorías: 920 Grasa Total: 63g Grasa Saturada: 10g Colesterol: 95mg Carbohidratos: 56g Azúcar: 30g Fibra: 9g Proteína: 38g Sodio: 310mg Vitamina A: 60% Vitamina C: 110% Calcio: 30% Hierro: 15%

Rinde 4 porciones

Esta ensalada combina hierbas frescas e ingredientes crujientes. Añade gajos de mandarina para endulzar esta fabulosa ensalada.

tailandesa de carne con tofu

12 oz/340g de tofu extra firme
6 tazas de vegetales/lechuga para ensalada, surtidos
½ taza de menta fresca
½ taza de albahaca fresca
1 pepino grande, pelado y en tajadas gruesas
1 cebolla roja, en cuatro partes
1 Cucharada de aceite de maní
8 oz/225g de bistec (falda o vacío), sin grasa
1 lata de 8 oz/225g de gajos de mandarina, escurridos
sal y pimienta
Aliño estilo Tailandés (ver página 90)

Cubre un plato con papel toalla. Retira el tofu de su empaque, escurre y corta en cubos de 1 pulgada; acomódalos sobre el papel toalla y deja escurrir por 30 minutos. Presiona suavemente escurriendo cualquier líquido restante con papel toalla.

Coloca la hoja en el **Quick Chef**, combina la cebolla y pepino y gira la manija picando grueso. En un tazón grande, combina la lechuga, menta, albahaca y la mezcla del pepino. Vierte la mitad de la vinagreta sobre la mezcla de lechuga y revuelve. Calienta la **Sartén Chef Series™ de 11"/28 cm** a fuego Mediano Alto. Añade el aceite de maní a la sartén. Añade la carne y cocina 3 minutos o hasta que la carne esté cocida a tu gusto. Retira la carne de la sartén y deja reposar 5 minutos sobre una tabla de cortar. Añade el tofu a la sartén caliente. Cocina el tofu hasta dorar ligeramente. Retira del fuego y reserva. Rebana la carne en tajadas finas y coloca en un tazón con la mezcla de lechuga. Añade el tofu y combina. Adorna con los gajos de mandarina.

Nota: Puedes reemplazar la carne por pollo sancochado o salmón.

Información Nutricional (por porción): Calorías: 270 Grasa Total:15g Grasa Saturada: 2.5g Colesterol: 30mg Carbohidratos:15g Azúcar: 7g Fibra: 4g Proteína: 22g Sodio: 400mg Vitamina A: 35% Vitamina C: 45% Calcio: 25% Hierro: 25%

Rinde 4 porciones

Pocas ensaladas superan una ensalada Cobb clásica. Esta ensalada combina todos los ingredientes tradicionales con una elegante vinagreta de champán.

"cobb" de pavo

- 2 Cucharadas de vinagre de champán
- 2 cucharaditas de mostaza Dijon
- 1 cucharadita de salsa Worcestershire
- ½ taza de mayonesa ligera
- ¼ taza de aceite de oliva extra virgen
- 4 oz/115g de queso Roquefort, desmenuzado
- ¾ taza o 6 tajadas de tocino previamente cocido, desmenuzado
- 1 bolsa de 10 oz/285g de vegetales/ lechuga para ensalada surtidos
- 1 aguacate pequeño pelado, sin semilla y en tajadas
- 4 tomates pequeños, picados
- ½ libra de pechuga de pavo, cortada en cubos
- sal y pimienta

En la base de la **Batidora Whip 'N Prep™**, coloca el vinagre de champán, mostaza Dijon, salsa Worcestershire, mayonesa y aceite de oliva. Coloca la cubierta y gira el asa mezclando bien. Reserva. Coloca el tocino en un plato seguro para colocar en el microondas y calienta por 1 minuto para que quede crujiente. Desmenuza y reserva. Coloca los vegetales surtidos en un tazón grande. Acomoda encima el tocino, aguacate, tomate y pavo. Rocía con el aliño y sirve.

Nota: Para una presentación tradicional, acomoda las tajadas de aguacate, tomate, pavo y tocino en hileras sobre los vegetales.

Información Nutricional (por porción): Calorías: 540 Grasa Total: 45g Grasa Saturada: 11g Colesterol: 65mg Carbohidratos: 18g Azúcar: 7g Fibra: 6g Proteína: 22g Sodio: 1420mg Vitamina A: 45% Vitamina C: 35% Calcio: 20% Hierro: 10%

Rinde 6 porciones

La ensalada de atún puede ser deliciosa y ligera. Esta versión incluye frijoles blancos y vegetales crujientes, resultando en una combinación cremosa y crujiente.

toscana de atún

- 2 tallos de apio
- ½ cebolla roja, en tajadas finas
- ½ taza de perejil
- 1 lata de 6 oz/170g de atún blanco, escurrido
- 1 lata de 15 oz/425g de frijoles blancos, enjuagados y escurridos
- ¾ taza de Vinagreta de Vino Rojo (ver página 90)
- sal y pimienta

Coloca el apio y perejil en la base del **Chef Picador Chop'N Prep™**. Hala el cordón, de 5 a 6 veces, picando finamente. Combina la mezcla del apio e ingredientes restantes en un tazón grande. Añade sal y pimienta al gusto. Sirve de inmediato o refrigera hasta por tres días.

Información Nutricional (por porción): Calorías: 250 Grasa Total: 19g Grasa Saturada: 2.5g Colesterol: 10mg Carbohidratos: 12g Azúcar: 2g Fibra: 3g Proteína: 11g Sodio: 230mg Vitamina A: 10% Vitamina C: 15% Calcio: 4% Hierro: 8%

ensaladas para niños saludables y felices

Tus pequeños quedarán fascinados con las divertidas ensaladas de esta sección. Diseñadas con ellos en mente, incluyen muchos ingredientes que sus paladares prefieren, pero nunca llegarán a saber que estos platos están llenos de saludables frutas y vegetales para que crezcan fuertes. Estas recetas aseguran barrigas llenas y corazones contentos.

"grandes ligas"

¡Tu pequeño deportista quedará encantado con esta nueva y divertida manera de comer salchichas después del partido! Para una opción baja en grasa, reemplaza las salchichas con salchichas de pavo.

Rinde 6 porciones

¼ taza salsa de tomate/ketchup
¼ taza de mayonesa con poca grasa
¼ taza de salsa dulce de pepinillos en vinagre/relish
1 Cucharada de mostaza en grano, entero
1 cucharadita de aceite vegetal
6 salchichas, en trozos de 1 pulgada
1 bolsa de 8 oz/225g mezcla para ensalada de col/coleslaw
1 bolsa de 10 oz/285g de lechuga surtida
4 tomates pequeños madurados en rama, picados
½ taza de pepinillos encurtidos/gherkin (pequeños), picados
sal y pimienta

Coloca en la base de la **Batidora Whip 'N Prep™**, la salsa de tomate, mayonesa, salsa dulce de pepinillos y mostaza. Tapa y gira la manija mezclando bien. Reserva o refrigera si no vas a usar inmediatamente.

Calienta el aceite vegetal en la **Sartén Chef Series para Freír de 11"/28 cm** sobre fuego Mediano-Alto. Añade los trozos de salchicha y cocina cinco minutos o hasta que se hayan calentado completamente.

En un tazón para servir, coloca la lechuga, la mezcla para ensalada de col, tomates, pepinillos encurtidos y el aliño que has preparado. Añade los trozos de salchicha. Sirve de inmediato.

Información Nutricional (por porción):
Calorías: 240 Grasa Total: 18g
Grasa Saturada: 6g Colesterol: 30mg
Carbohidratos: 15g Azúcar: 10g
Fibra: 2g Proteína: 16g Sodio: 890mg
Vitamina A: 30% Vitamina C: 40%
Calcio: 4% Hierro: 6%

macarrones con *ranch* cremoso

Una alternativa ligera y bien balanceada al plato tradicional de macarrones con queso. Esta ensalada de pasta usa aliño Ranch hecho en casa y divertidos estilos de pasta que encantarán a tus niños.

Rinde 8 porciones

8 oz/225g de pasta de rueditas o algún diseño pequeño, cruda
bolsa de 1 libra/455g de vegetales surtidos, congelados
1 pimiento rojo pequeño, en cuatro partes
2 tazas de pollo (cocido en la **Vaporera Inteligente Tupperware®** o pollo a la brasa), picado
Aliño Ranch Ligero (ver pág. 89)
sal y pimienta negra

Acomoda los vegetales congelados en la Base Vaporera de la **Vaporera Inteligente Tupperware®**. Cocina al microondas, en Potencia Alta, por 10 minutos. Retira la Base Vaporera y enjuaga los vegetales en agua fría para detener la cocción. Hierve 2 Cuartos/1.8 L de agua con sal en la **Olla Chef Series™ de 3 Cuartos/ 2.8 L**. Añade la pasta y cocina 9 minutos o hasta que esté al dente. Escurre la pasta y enfría completamente bajo agua fría. Coloca el pimiento rojo en la base del **Chef Picador Chop 'N Prep™**. Coloca la cubierta y hala el cordón, de 2 a 3 veces, hasta picar grueso. Coloca la pasta, pollo, vegetales y pimiento rojo en un tazón grande. Revuelve con el aliño, sal y pimienta negra al gusto.

Información Nutricional (por porción): Calorías: 260
Grasa Total: 6g Grasa Saturada: 2g Colesterol: 40mg
Carbohidratos: 32g Azúcar: 5g Fibra: 2g Proteína: 17g
Sodio: 120mg Vitamina A: 30% Vitamina C: 30%
Calcio: 6% Hierro: 8%

pollitos empanizados

En vez de papitas fritas, sirve los medallones de pollo empanizados sobre esta alegre ensalada de lechuga y queso cheddar. ¡El aliño deliciosamente ácido hace de esta ensalada un "gol"!

Rinde 6 porciones

½ taza de mayonesa ligera
2 Cucharadas de miel
2 Cucharadas de mostaza amarilla
2 cucharadas de jugo de limón
1 bolsa de 8 oz/225g de lechuga picada para tacos
1 bolsa de 8 oz/225g para ensalada de col
1 taza de mini pretzels crujientes
1 taza de queso cheddar rallado
1 taza de tomates aperitivo, por la mitad
6 medallones de pollo empanizados y listos, cortados en trozos
sal y pimienta

En la base de la **Batidora Whip 'N Prep™**, coloca la mayonesa, miel, mostaza y jugo de limón. Tapa y gira la manija hasta mezclar bien. Reserva o refrigera si no vas a usar de inmediato. En un tazón grande, combina la lechuga, mezcla para col y el aderezo. Adorna con pretzels, queso, tomates y pollo. Sirve de inmediato.

Nota: Puedes comprar los trozos de pollo empanizados en la sección "deli" o en la sección de alimentos refrigerados o congelados de tu almacén.

Información Nutricional (por porción): Calorías: 350
Grasa Total: 20g Grasa Saturada: 6g Colesterol: 50mg
Carbohidratos: 26g Azúcar: 10g Fibra: 3g Proteína: 18g
Sodio: 770mg Vitamina A: 15% Vitamina C: 40%
Calcio: 15% Hierro: 6%

anaranjada

Una delicia para toda la familia. Esta ensalada está cargada de vitamina A y C, ayudando a tus niños a desarrollar buena vista y huesos saludables.

Rinde 4 porciones

1 bolsa de 10 oz/285g de zanahorias picadas en palitos bien finos *o*
10 oz/285g de zanahorias ralladas con el **Rallador Grate 'N Measure™**
1 taza de arándanos secos
1 Cucharada de semillas de amapola
1 lata de 8 oz/225g de trocitos y jugo de piña
½ taza de jugo de naranja
sal y pimienta

Coloca las zanahorias picadas o ralladas en la base del **Quick Chef**, y gira el asa para picar rápidamente en trozos pequeños. Combina todos los ingredientes en un tazón de servir. Refrigera varias horas dejando que tome sabor. Sirve frío.

Información Nutricional (por porción): Calorías: 180
Grasa Total: 1.5g Grasa Saturada: 0g Colesterol: 0mg
Carbohidratos: 43g Azúcar: 32g Fibra: 5g Proteína: 1g
Sodio: 55mg Vitamina A: 240% Vitamina C: 45%
Calcio: 6% Hierro: 4%

aliños

Es fácil y divertido preparar aliños frescos para ensalada. Sea un ranch cremoso o una sabrosa vinagreta, preparar tus aliños en casa te ahorra dinero y añade un sabor fresco a tus ensaladas. Estos aliños varían de sabor y de inspiración cultural. Usa tu imaginación para probar diferentes ensaladas con diferentes aliños, logrando cada vez un nuevo resultado de sabor.

albahaca

Rinde ½ taza

½ taza de hojas de albahaca fresca
2 Cucharadas de vinagre balsámico
1 Cucharada de miel
½ taza de aceite de oliva
sal y pimienta

Coloca las hojas de albahaca fresca en la base del **Chef Picador Chop 'N Prep™**. Hala el cordón, de 4 a 5 veces, para picar. Añade la albahaca, vinagre balsámico, miel, aceite de oliva, sal y pimienta al **Recipiente Quick Shake®**. Coloca la cubierta y sacude hasta incorporar bien.

Información Nutricional (por porción):
Calorías: 280 Grasa Total: 28g
Grasa Saturada: 4g Colesterol: 0mg
Carbohidratos: 6g Azúcar: 6g Fibra: 0g
Proteína: 0g Sodio:0mg

cilantro y lima

Rinde 2 tazas

1 taza de consomé de vegetales
1½ cucharadita de arrurruz en polvo o maicena
½ taza de jugo fresco de lima
½ cucharadita de azúcar
2 Cucharadas de aceite de ajonjolí
¼ taza de aceite de maní
2 Cucharadas de aceite de canola
2 Cucharadas de sal marina
1 cucharadita de cilantro

Combina el espesante (arrurruz o maicena) con 1½ cucharaditas del consomé frío y mezcla formando una pasta. Haz hervir el resto del consomé en una olla pequeña y añade la mezcla del espesante con el consomé. Hierve hasta que espese, unos 2 minutos. Retira del fuego y deja enfriar. Añade jugo de lima y azúcar y revuelve para combinar. Deja enfriar completamente en el refrigerador o sobre un tazón con hielo. Coloca la mezcla fría en el **Recipiente Quick Shake®**. Añade aceite, coloca el sello y sacude bien. Añade la sal y el cilantro.

Información Nutricional (por porción):
Calorías: 70 Grasa Total: 7g
Grasa Saturada: 1g Colesterol: 0mg
Carbohidratos: 1g Azúcar: 1g Fibra: 0g
Proteína: 0g Sodio: 710mg

griego

Rinde ½ taza de aliño

4 Cucharadas de jugo de limón
2 dientes de ajo, picados
¼ taza de aceite de oliva extra virgen

Coloca todos los ingredientes en el **Recipiente Quick Shake®**. Coloca la cubierta y sacude hasta combinar bien.

Información Nutricional (por porción):
Calorías: 130 Grasa Total: 14g
Grasa Saturada: 2g Colesterol: 0mg
Carbohidratos: 2mg Azúcar: 0mg
Fibra: 0g Proteína: 0g Sodio: 0mg

mostaza con miel

Rinde ¾ tazas

½ taza de mayonesa *ligera*
2 Cucharadas de miel
2 Cucharadas de mostaza amarilla
2 Cucharadas de jugo de limón
sal y pimienta

En la base de la Batidora Whip 'N Prep™, coloca la mayonesa, miel, mostaza, jugo de limón y sazonadores. Coloca la cubierta y gira la manija, mezclando bien.

Información Nutricional (por porción):
Calorías: 80 Grasa Total: 6g
Grasa Saturada: 1g Colesterol: 5mg
Carbohidratos: 7g Azúcar: 6g Fibra: 0g
Proteína: 0g Sodio: 160mg

ranch ligero

Rinde ¾ tazas

½ taza de leche agria/*buttermilk*
½ taza de crema agria *ligera*
¼ taza de mayonesa *ligera*
1 Cucharada de jugo de limón
1 Cucharada de cebollines deshidratados/chives
1 diente de ajo
sal y pimienta

Coloca el ajo y los cebollines deshidratados en el **Chef Picador Chop 'N Prep™**. Coloca la cubierta y hala el cordón, de 4 a 5 veces, picando finamente. Añade la leche agria, crema agria y mayonesa en la base de la **Batidora Whip 'N Prep™**. Con el **Exprimidor Tupperware® de Lima-Limón**, escurre el limón en el recipiente, añade el ajo y los cebollines. Coloca de nuevo la cubierta y gira el asa mezclando bien.

Información Nutricional (por porción):
Calorías: 35 Grasa Total: 3g
Grasa Saturada: 1g Colesterol: 5mg
Carbohidratos: 2g Azúcar: 1g Fibra: 0g
Proteína:1g Sodio: 40mg

maní

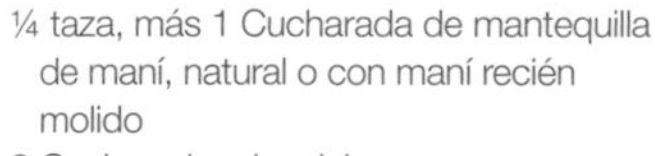

Rinde 1 1/8 taza

¼ taza, más 1 Cucharada de mantequilla de maní, natural o con maní recién molido
2 Cucharadas de miel
1 cucharadita de salsa de soja
¼ taza de vinagre de arroz
¼ taza de aceite canola
1 Cucharada de aceite de ajonjolí
2 Cucharadas de agua tibia
sal y pimienta

Combina todos los ingredientes en la base de la **Batidora Whip 'N Prep™**. Coloca la cubierta y bate hasta que la mezcla esté suave. Almacena refrigerado hasta por 1 semana.

Información Nutricional (por porción):
Calorías: 130 Grasa Total: 12g
Grasa Saturada: 1.5g Colesterol: 0mg
Carbohidratos: 6g Azúcar: 5g Fibra: 1g
Proteína: 2g Sodio: 80mg

pesto

Rinde ¾ taza

2/3 taza de pesto preparado
2 Cucharadas de vinagre de vino blanco
3 Cucharadas de aceite de oliva extra virgen
sal y pimienta

Coloca el pesto, vinagre, sal y pimienta en el **Recipiente Quick Shake®**. Añade el aceite de oliva, coloca el sello y sacude hasta que los ingredientes estén bien incorporados.

Información Nutricional (por porción):
Calorías: 210 Grasa Total: 22g
Grasa Saturada: 3.5g Colesterol: 0mg
Carbohidratos: 1g Azúcar: 0g Fibra: 0g
Proteína: 2g Sodio: 40mg

salsa pesto

Rinde 2/3 taza

¾ taza de hojas de albahaca, bien compactas
3 Cucharadas de piñones, tostados
1 diente de ajo
¼ taza de queso Parmesano rallado
½ taza de aceite de oliva extra virgen
sal y pimienta

Coloca la albahaca, piñones, ajo, queso Parmesano y aceite en la base del **Chef Picador Chop 'N Prep™**. Coloca la cubierta, gira para sellar y hala el cordón, de 4 a 5 veces, hasta picar finamente. Sazona con sal y pimienta.

Información Nutricional (por porción):
Calorías: 160 Grasa Total: 17g
Grasa Saturada: 2.5g Colesterol: 0mg
Carbohidratos: 1g Azúcar: 0g Fibra: 0g
Proteína: 2g Sodio: 40mg

semilla de amapola

Rinde ¾ taza

½ taza de mayonesa
2 Cucharadas de miel
½ Cucharada de mostaza Dijon
1 Cucharada de vinagre de sidra de manzana
2 Cucharadas de jugo de limón
½ Cucharada de semillas de amapola
sal y pimienta

Añade todos los ingredientes a la base del **Recipiente Quick Shake®**. Reemplaza la cubierta y sacude hasta combinar bien.

Información Nutricional (por porción):
Calorías: 90 Grasa Total: 7g
Grasa Saturada: 1g Colesterol: 5mg
Carbohidratos: 8g Azúcar: 7g Fibra: 0g
Proteína: 0g Sodio: 260mg

vino rojo y frambuesa

Rinde 1 taza

¼ taza de vinagre de vino rojo y frambuesa
¾ taza de aceite de oliva
1 cucharadita de mostaza Dijon
2 dientes de ajo, molidos
sal y pimienta

Añade todos los ingredientes en el **Recipiente Quick Shake®**. Coloca el sello y sacude, combinando bien.

Información Nutricional (por porción):
Calorías: 190 Grasa Total: 21g
Grasa Saturada: 3g Colesterol: 0mg
Carbohidratos: 0g Azúcar: 0g Fibra: 0g
Proteína: 0g Sodio: 15mg

vino rojo

Rinde ¾ taza

¼ taza de vinagre de vino rojo
2 Cucharadas de jugo de limón
1 cucharadita de miel
½ taza de aceite de oliva extra virgen
sal y pimienta

Añade todos los ingredientes en el **Recipiente Quick Shake®**. Coloca el sello y sacude, combinando bien.

Información Nutricional (por porción):
Calorías: 170 Grasa Total: 19g
Grasa Saturada: 2.5g Colesterol: 0mg
Carbohidratos: 1g Azúcar: 1g Fibra: 0g
Proteína: 0g Sodio: 0mg

picante

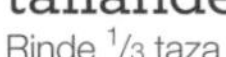

Rinde 1 1/8 taza

½ cucharadita de pimienta de cayena
¼ taza de vinagre de vino blanco
1 cucharadita de sal
1 cucharadita de mostaza en polvo
2½ cucharaditas de azúcar
1 cucharadita de ajo en polvo
10–12 gotas de salsa picante
¾ de taza de aceite vegetal

Combina todos los ingredientes, excepto el aceite vegetal, en el **Recipiente Quick Shake®**. Sacude vigorosamente hasta combinar bien. Retira el sello de tapita, añade el aceite vegetal, coloca el sello y sacude hasta incorporar bien

Información Nutricional (por porción):
Calorías: 170 Grasa Total: 18g
Grasa Saturada: 1.5g Colesterol: 0mg
Carbohidratos: 2g Azúcar: 1g Fibra: 0g
Proteína: 0g Sodio: 270mg

agridulce

Rinde 1 taza

½ taza de aceite canola
½ taza de azúcar
¼ taza de vinagre de sidra de manzana
sal y pimienta

Coloca todos los ingredientes en el **Recipiente Quick Shake®**. Sella y sacude bien, hasta combinar completamente.

Información Nutricional (por porción):
Calorías: 140 Grasa Total: 11g
Grasa Saturada: 1g Colesterol: 0mg
Carbohidratos: 10g Azúcar: 10g Fibra: 0g
Proteína: 0g Sodio: 60mg

tailandés

Rinde 1/3 taza

½ pimiento jalapeño, sin semillas
¼ taza de jugo de lima
1 Cucharada de salsa para pescado, estilo tailandés
2 cucharaditas de aceite de ajonjolí
½ cucharadita de azúcar

Con el **Cuchillo Utilitario Chef Series™ Pro**, pica el jalapeño finamente. Añade el jalapeño, la lima, la salsa de pescado, el aceite de ajonjolí y el azúcar al **Recipiente Quick Shake®**. Coloca la cubierta y sacude, combinando bien.

Información Nutricional (por porción):
Calorías: 30 Grasa Total: 2.5g
Grasa Saturada: 0g Colesterol: 0mg
Carbohidratos:2g Azúcar: 1g Fibra: 0g
Proteína: 0g Sodio: 350mg

sensationnelles

salades

pour votre famille et vous-même

"Qu'était le Paradis sinon un jardin rempli de fruits, de légumes, de fines herbes et de plaisirs; rien que des délices."
- William Lawson

table des matières

C’est facile de s’extasier à propos d'un bifteck juteux ou d'un dessert décadent, mais une salade mémorable est un véritable succès. Des légumes mûrs, de la laitue croquante, des motifs colorés et des vinaigrettes savoureuses se combinent pour donner un plat vraiment excitant. Que ce soit un accompagnement ou un plat principal ou une alternative à un souper copieux, les salades sont le vecteur ultime pour les cuisiniers imaginatifs.

Le contenant Salade-santé à emporter de Tupperware est parfait pour emporter la fraîcheur avec soi partout où on va. Avec trois caractéristiques distinctes, ce produit est un bar à salades mobile, prêt quand vous êtes prêt.

Le contenant arbore un couvercle virtuellement hermétique et étanche afin que vous n’ayez pas à vous soucier des fuites ou de l'altération du contenu. Le couvercle abrite une fourchette et un couteau-pression innovateurs, et un petit contenant virtuellement hermétique et étanche s'y loge confortablement pour abriter les vinaigrettes qui ne flétriront pas votre salade. Quand vous êtes prêt/e à manger, versez la vinaigrette sur la verdure fraîche pour une option de déjeuner sain et rafraîchissant.

Ce livre de recettes présente 24 salades et 13 vinaigrettes à combiner. Des combinaisons d’inspiration thaï aux salades de pâtes, ces créations fraîches ont été conçues pour votre famille et vous-même. Bon appétit!

Jeunes épinards
Ils sont portés aux nues comme un choix sain, mais avec leur couleur vert foncé et leur saveur douce, c'est aussi un pur délice.

Roquette
La roquette épicée a de longues feuilles et une saveur qui rappelle les épices et les herbes aromatiques. C'est un amour de laitue à marier avec des salades fruitées sucrées.

Romaine
Rendue célèbre par la classique salade César, la romaine va des feuilles claires proches du coeur aux feuilles foncées à l'extérieur, pleines de croquant et de fraîcheur.

Boston (Bibb ou beurre)
Délicate et raffinée, cette laitue offre une alternative à l'iceberg en dégageant une subtilité sucrée.

Mélange printanier
Si vous optez pour un mélange de salades en sachet, c'est l'idéal. Une combinaison de saveurs, de couleurs et de textures qui suscite le plaisir des yeux et flatte le palais.

fabuleuse verdure

Une salade, c'est bien plus que l'éternelle et classique laitue iceberg. Variez les plaisirs en essayant la roquette épicée ou la Boston au goût raffiné, la prochaine fois que vous emportez une salade bonne pour la santé.

Laitue à feuilles rouges
Dans les tons dramatiques de marron, la laitue à feuilles rouges ajoute une note de couleur dans l'assiette et se caractérise par sa saveur douce, similaire à la laitue à feuilles vertes.

Laitue à feuilles vertes
Des feuilles plissées et une saveur presque douce font de cette laitue une favorite des amateurs de salade. Une excellente alternative à la romaine ou la salade iceberg du fait de sa neutralité.

Radicchio
Le radicchio de couleur rouge foncé est fabuleux sur le gril, qui fait ressortir son goût légèrement amer. Mélangé à d'autres verdures, le radicchio offre un contraste complexe.

Iceberg
La classique iceberg (batavia américaine) est croquante, rafraîchissante et se garde bien au réfrigérateur pendant des semaines si elle est conservée comme il faut.

Chou Nappa (chou chinois)
Ce membre de la famille du chou se caractérise par ses feuilles longues, larges, froissées et sa saveur douce.

Frisée (voir page 100)
Cette laitue française unique a d'élégantes feuilles découpées et frisées et une saveur légèrement amère qui se marie particulièrement bien avec des éléments crémeux comme le jaune d'oeuf ou la vinaigrette veloutée.

spectaculaires salades d'accompagnement

Il n'est pas nécessaire de recourir aux plats d'accompagnement monochromes; ces salades pourraient bien être le clou du repas. Une salade bien composée peut ajouter un intérêt visuel et une saveur complexe à un repas. Servir un repas mémorable est aussi facile que combiner des ingrédients frais et des saveurs excitantes avec une bonne nutrition. Pour une fois, laissez de côté le brocoli à la vapeur et préparez plutôt une salade facile et délicieuse.

Donne 4 portions

Une délicieuse alternative au riz nature, cette salade incorpore des olives kalamata, du maïs et des oignons verts pour une couleur et une saveur qui impressionneront à coup sûr.

salade de riz basmati

1 tasse de riz Basmati
2 tasses d'eau
⅓ tasse d'huile de canola
3 c. à soupe de vinaigre de vin blanc
1 c. à thé de moutarde de Dijon
1 c. à thé de miel
¼ c. à thé de gingembre en poudre
1 tasse de maïs frais ou congelé, cuit
2 oignons verts, hachés
½ tasse de noix de cajou, hachées
1 tasse d'olives Kalamata dénoyautées, hachées
sel et poivre

Combiner le riz et 2 tasses d'eau dans un **Cuit-riz micro-ondes Tupperware®**. Remettre le couvercle et cuire aux micro-ondes sur Fort pendant 5 minutes. Puis, cuire aux micro-ondes sur Moyen pendant 15 minutes. Laisser reposer 5 minutes. Aérer avec une cuiller de service et mettre de côté.

Pour faire la vinaigrette, combiner l'huile, le vinaigre, la moutarde, le miel et le gingembre dans un **Mélangeur rapide**. Assaisonner de sel et de poivre. Mettre de côté.

Pour assembler la salade, combiner le riz cuit, la vinaigrette et le reste des ingrédients dans un grand bol. Remuer le tout et servir chaud, à température ambiante, ou froid.

Valeur nutritive (par portion) : Calories : 250 Total lipides : 15 g Lipides saturés : 1,5 g Cholestérol : 0 mg Glucides : 28 g Sucres : 1 g Fibres : 2 g Protéines : 4 g Sodium : 190 mg Vitamine A : 3 % Vitamine C : 5 % Calcium : 3 % Fer : 7 %

Donne 4 portions

Servez cette salade légère l'été quand les tomates et le basilic sont au pic de la fraîcheur.

salade de capri

8 oz/225 g de mozzarella fraîche, dans l'eau
6 petites tomates mûries sur pied
Vinaigrette au basilic (page 111)
½ tasse de feuilles de basilic frais
set et poivre

À l'aide d'un **Couteau tout usage dentelé de la Série Chef^MC Pro**, trancher les tomates et la mozzarella fraîche en rondelles. Superposer les tranches de tomate, le basilic frais et la mozzarella pour servir. Arroser de Vinaigrette au basilic et assaisonner de sel et poivre, au goût.

Remarque : La salade de Capri restante peut s'ajouter à des pâtes ou être mélangée à de la verdure pour une salade composée.

Valeur nutritive (par portion) : Calories : 470 Total lipides : 41 g Lipides saturés : 11 g Cholestérol : 45 mg Glucides : 13 g Sucres : 10 g Fibres : 2 g Protéines : 14 g Sodium : 360 mg Vitamine A : 40 % Vitamine C : 30 % Calcium : 30 % Fer : 6 %

Donne 6 portions

Ce ceviche à la mexicaine est délicieux pour un pique-nique en plein air ou un barbecue, car il constitue un complément plus léger aux viandes grillées.

ceviche veracruz

1 lb/455 g de crevettes, pelées et déveinées (sans la queue)
jus de 2 citrons
jus de 2 limes
jus de 2 oranges
1 concombre, épépiné et épluché
½ tasse d'oignon rouge, épluché et haché
2 piments jalapeno, épépinés
1 tomate, épépinée
1 avocat, dénoyauté
¼ tasse de coriandre
sel et poivre

Mélanger les crevettes avec la moitié du jus des agrumes et les mettre dans **l'Intelli-Vap Tupperware®**. Remplir le réservoir avec 1 ¾ tasse d'eau. Mettre au four à micro-ondes sur Fort pendant 7 minutes. Retirer du four à micro-ondes, mettre les crevettes dans le **Rapido-chef**, avec la lame, et hacher grossièrement. Transférer dans un grand bol. Ajouter les jus d'agrumes restants dans le bol. Mettre de côté.

Mettre le concombre, l'oignon et le piment dans la base du **Rapido-chef** et hacher grossièrement. Transférer dans le bol avec les crevettes. Mettre la tomate, l'avocat et la coriandre dans la base du **Rapido-chef** et tourner la manivelle pour hacher grossièrement. Ajouter dans le bol. Remuer pour combiner les ingrédients, assaisonner au goût. Servir avec des croustilles de tortilla, si désiré.

Valeur nutritive (par portion) : Calories : 150 Total lipides : 6 g Lipides saturés : 1 g Cholestérol : 110 mg Glucides : 11 g Sucres : 5 g Fibres : 3 g Protéines : 14 g Sodium : 135 mg Vitamine A : 10 % Vitamine C : 60 % Calcium : 4 % Fer : 10 %

Donne 4 portions

Cette salade doit sa longévité à la combinaison parfaite d'ingrédients frais de haute qualité. Les croustilles de pita sont parfaites pour prendre le dernier cube de fromage feta.

salade grecque avec croustilles de pita chaude

4 galettes de pain pita, coupées en 4
½ c. à thé d'origan déshydraté
1 c. à thé d'huile d'olive extra vierge
10 oz/285 g de salade romaine
1 concombre
1 tomate
1 tasse d'olives noires
2 oignons verts
½ tasse de Vinaigrette grecque (voir page 111)
¾ tasse de fromage feta émietté

Préchauffer le four à 350° F/175° C.

Mettre le pain pita sur une plaque pour le four. L'arroser d'huile d'olive. Saupoudrer d'origan déshydraté, de sel et de poivre. Mettre au four pendant 10 minutes, ou jusqu'à ce que la pita soit croustillante.

Pendant que la pita grille, assembler la salade. Ajouter le concombre, la tomate, les olives et les oignons verts dans la base du **Rapido-chef**. Tourner la manivelle pour hacher grossièrement. Combiner les feuilles de salade, le concombre, la tomate, les olives et les oignons verts. Remuer avec ¼ tasse de vinaigrette. Garnir de fromage et de pita chaude. Servir immédiatement.

Valeur nutritive (par portion) : Calories : 280 Total lipides : 16 g Lipides saturés : 4 g Cholestérol : 10 mg Glucides : 27 g Sucres : 3 g Fibres : 6 g Protéines : 10 g Sodium : 830 mg Vitamine A : 140 % Vitamine C : 45 % Calcium : 15 % Fer : 15 %

Donne 6 portions

Cette salade est très française, et vous pouvez la trouver dans les bistros du tout Paris. La frisée amère est complétée par le fromage de chèvre piquant et un oeuf poché crémeux.

salade bistro parisienne

- 1 baguette, coupée en 20 tranches
- 5 oz/140 g de fromage de chèvre
- 1 tête de laitue frisée
- ½ tasse de noix hachées
- poivre noir
- 6 oeufs, pochés ou frits
- Vinaigrette revigorante (voir page 112)

Préchauffer le gril du four. Trancher la baguette avec le **Couteau à pain de la Série ChefMC Pro**. Utiliser un **Couteau à éplucher de la Série ChefMC Pro** pour couper le fromage de chèvre en tranches fines. Mettre une tranche de fromage sur chaque tranche de pain pour faire un croûton. Saupoudrer de poivre noir, si désiré. Mettre sous le gril et faire griller jusqu'à ce que le fromage soit doré. Mettre les feuilles de frisée sur des assiettes à salade, garnir avec l'oeuf, 2–3 croûtons et saupoudrer de noix.

Valeur nutritive (par portion) : Calories : 590 Total lipides : 40 g Lipides saturés : 6 g Cholestérol : 45 mg Glucides : 45 g Sucres : 3 g Fibres : 5 g Protéines : 16 g Sodium : 950 mg Vitamine A : 45 % Vitamine C : 10 % Calcium : 10 % Fer : 20 %

Donne 5 portions

Le quinoa est une céréale complète et une bonne source de protéines et d'acides aminés qui peuvent aider le système immunitaire et la santé en général. Le subtil arôme d'orange donne à cette salade d'accompagnement une élégance supplémentaire.

salade de haricots noirs et quinoa

- 1 tasse de quinoa
- 1 ½ tasse de bouillon de poulet sans gras
- ½ tasse de jus d'orange fraîchement pressé
- 1 c. à soupe de zeste d'orange râpé
- ⅓ tasse d'huile d'olive extra vierge
- 2 gousses d'ail, émincées
- Jus d'une lime
- ¼ tasse de coriandre, hachée
- 1 c. à soupe de moutarde de Dijon
- 1 c. à soupe de Mélange Simple Indulgence™ Chipotle du Sud-ouest
- 1 petit poivron jaune, en quartiers
- 2 tomates moyenne mûries sur pied, hachées
- 15 oz/425 g de haricots noirs (en boîte), égouttés
- 1 petit poivron rouge, épépiné et coupé en gros morceaux
- sel et poivre

Combiner le quinoa, le bouillon de poulet, le jus et le zeste d'orange dans un **Cuit-riz micro-ondes Tupperware®**. Remettre le couvercle et cuire aux micro-ondes sur Fort pendant 15–18 minutes. Aérer avec une cuiller de service. Mettre l'huile d'olive, l'ail, le jus de lime, la coriandre, la moutarde de Dijon et le mélange pour assaisonnement dans un **Mélangeur rapide**. Remettre le couvercle et bien agiter pour combiner. Mettre les poivrons rouge et jaune dans la base du **Hachoir Gagne-temps.** Remettre le couvercle et tirer sur la corde 2–3 fois pour hacher grossièrement. Mettre les poivrons et le reste des ingrédients avec le quinoa cuit dans un grand bol. Remuer les légumes et le quinoa avec la vinaigrette. Assaisonner avec du sel et du poivre au goût.

Valeur nutritive (par portion) : Calories : 340 Total lipides : 17 g Lipides saturés : 2,5 g Cholestérol : 30 mg Glucides : 40 g Sucres : 7 g Fibres : 6 g Protéines : 10 g Sodium : 610 mg Vitamine A : 2 % Vitamine C : 40 % Calcium : 4 % Fer : 15 %

Donne 4 portions

Si vous rêvez de fromages bleus, craquez pour ce qui est bon. Les fromages bleus Maytag et danois figurent parmi les meilleurs et il n'en faut qu'un peu.

salade épinards et poire

1 paquet de petits épinards tendres
2 poires Anjou, épluchées, évidées et tranchées
½ tasse de moitiés de noix
½ tasse de miettes de Gorgonzola ou de bleu
Vinaigrette aux graines de pavots (voir page 112)

Mettre les épinards et les poires dans un grand bol. Mettre les noix dans la base du **Rapido-chef**. Remettre le couvercle et tourner la manivelle pour hacher grossièrement. Ajouter aux feuilles d'épinards et poires tranchées. Parsemer de fromage. Arroser de vinaigrette et remuer légèrement pour combiner.

Valeur nutritive (par portion) : Calories : 340 Total lipides : 23 g Lipides saturés : 5 g Cholestérol : 25 mg Glucides : 31 g Sucres : 19 g Fibres : 6 g Protéines : 8 g Sodium : 630 mg Vitamine A : 120 % Vitamine C : 40 % Calcium : 20 % Fer : 15 %

Donne 4 portions

Les fraises sont meilleures de mars à août, de sorte que cette salade est un suprême délice de nuit d'été. Le tofu, le poulet ou le bifteck grillé et tranché font de cette salade un plat à part entière.

salade fraises et épinards

½ lb de fraises tranchées
10 oz/285 g de petits épinards tendres
4 oz/115 g de fromage de chèvre émietté
2 c. à soupe de pignons, grillés
Vinaigrette miel-moutarde (voir page 111)

Dans un bol moyen, combiner les fraises et les petits épinards. Saupoudrer de fromage de chèvre émietté et de pignons grillés. Arroser avec votre vinaigrette favorite.

Valeur nutritive (par portion) : Calories : 190 Total lipides : 13 g Lipides saturés : 7 g Cholestérol : 30 mg Glucides : 8 g Sucres : 4 g Fibres : 3 g Protéines : 12 g Sodium : 150 mg Vitamine A : 130 % Vitamine C : 90 % Calcium : 35 % Fer :15 %

Donne 8 portions

Une petite cuillérée de vraie crème fouettée fait toute la différence dans cette version de salade de fruits des îles. Les amandes et flocons de noix de coco ajoutent du croquant et une saveur exotique.

salade de fruits d'été

- 2 tasses de cantaloup (melon brodé)
- 2 tasses de pastèque
- 1 lb/455 g de fraises, équeutées
- 2 kiwis, épluchés
- 1 tasse de crème épaisse
- 2 c. à soupe de sucre semoule
- 1 c. à thé d'extrait de rhum, facultatif
- ½ tasse de noix de coco en flocons, grillée
- ½ tasse d'amandes tranchées, grillées

Avec le **Couteau de chef de la Série Chef^MC Pro**, couper tous les fruits et les mettre dans un bol moyen. Mettre la crème épaisse dans la base du **Batteur Gagne-temps**; remettre le couvercle et tourner la manivelle pour fouetter jusqu'à ce que la crème commence à épaissir. Ajouter le sucre et l'extrait, et battre jusqu'à ce que des pics fermes se forment. Saupoudrer les fruits de noix de coco et d'amandes; garnir de crème fouettée. Servir immédiatement.

Valeur nutritive (par portion) : Calories : 240 Total lipides : 16 g Lipides saturés : 9 g Cholestérol : 40 mg Glucides : 23 g Sucres : 16 g Fibres : 4 g Protéines : 4 g Sodium : 20 mg Vitamine A : 45 % Vitamine C : 170 % Calcium : 6 % Fer : 6 %

Donne 6 portions

Inspirée par un voyage à Hawaï, cette salade est un mélange de pré et marée, combinant des saveurs tropicales pour une expérience unique.

salade de crevettes aux fruits

- 1 lb/455 g de crevettes cuites, pelées et déveinées
- 1 ananas, épluché, débarrassé du trognon et coupé en morceaux
- 2 mangues, épluchées et coupées en morceaux
- 2 bananes, en tranches
- 1 c. à soupe de noix de coco râpée, grillée
- 1 c. à soupe de noix de cajou, grillées et hachées
- 2 c. à soupe d'huile de canola
- 2 c. à soupe de café filtré
- 1 c. à soupe de sauce soja faible en sodium
- 1 lime, zeste et jus
- 2 c. à soupe de lait de coco léger
- 1 piment habañero, épépiné et haché finement
- ½ tasse de coriandre, hachée
- 1 c. à thé de gingembre frais, émincé
- sel et poivre, au goût

6 tasses de roquette, facultatif

Mettre les crevettes, l'ananas, les mangues, les bananes, la noix de coco et les noix de cajou dans un grand bol Remuer pour combiner. Ajouter l'huile, le café, la sauce soja, le jus de lime et le lait de noix de coco dans la base d'un **Mélangeur rapide** et mettre de côté. Mettre le piment habanero, la coriandre et le gingembre dans le **Hachoir Gagne-temps** et tirer sur la corde 4-5 fois ou jusqu'à ce qu'ils soient hachés finement. Ajouter dans le Mélangeur rapide, remettre le couvercle et agiter jusqu'à ce que le tout soit bien combiné. Verser la vinaigrette sur les crevettes et les fruits et mettre au frais au réfrigérateur au moins 1 heure. Servir sur de la roquette, si désiré.

Valeur nutritive (par portion) : Calories : 290 Total lipides : 7 g Lipides saturés : 1 g Cholestérol : 145 mg Glucides : 43 g Sucres : 30 g Fibres : 5 g Protéines : 18 g Sodium : 240 mg Vitamine A : 20 % Vitamine C : 180 % Calcium : 6 % Fer : 20 %

salades en plat principal

Les salades peuvent combler l'appétit. Essayez une de ces merveilles en plat principal. Combinez des laitues croquantes avec des fruits et légumes colorés et ajoutez une bonne source de protéine pour une salade rassasiante qui ne vous alourdira pas. Ajoutez des haricots riches en nutriments, du tofu, du porc, du bifteck, du poisson ou du poulet à pratiquement toutes les salades pour un plat principal qui exalte les sens.

Donne 8 portions

Du cari fumé et des morceaux de mangue fraîche complètent les qualités naturelles de cette fantastique version d'une salade de poulet classique.

salade de poulet bombay à la mangue

- 1/3 tasse de yogourt grec nature non gras
- 1/3 tasse de mayonnaise non grasse
- 1 c. à soupe de poudre de cari
- 3 c. à soupe de jus de lime
- 1 c. à soupe de miel
- 3 poitrines de poulet (pochées ou cuites à la vapeur dans **l'Intelli-Vap Tupperware®**), en dés
- 1 mangue mûre, épluchée, débarrassée de son noyau et hachée
- 1 tasse de raisins rouges sans pépins, coupés en deux
- 8 oz/225 g de châtaignes d'eau en boîte, égouttées
- ½ tasse de noix de cajou salées, grillées
- sel et poivre

Dans votre grand bol favori ou **Batteur Gagne-temps**, fouetter ensemble le yogourt, la mayonnaise, la poudre de cari, le jus de lime et le miel. Ajouter le reste des ingrédients et remuer délicatement avec la vinaigrette. Servir immédiatement ou réfrigérer pendant trois jours maximum

Valeur nutritive (par portion) : Calories : 190 Total lipides : 8 g Lipides saturés : 1,5 g Cholestérol : 30 mg Glucides : 17 g Sucres : 11 g Fibres : 2 g Protéines : 13 g Sodium : 120 mg Vitamine A : 4 % Vitamine C : 20 % Calcium : 2 % Fer : 8 %

Donne 6 portions

Le croquant de la laitue fraîche complète les noix de cajou crémeuses et les saveurs asiatiques authentiques de ces roulés de laitue amusants à manger.

lits de laitue poulet-cajou

- 1 tête de laitue iceberg ou Bibb
- 3 poitrines de poulet (pochées ou cuites à la vapeur dans **l'Intelli-Vap Tupperware®**)
- 1 c. à thé d'huile de sésame
- ½ oignon jaune, haché
- Morceau de 1 pouce de gingembre frais
- 6 gousses d'ail
- ¾ tasse de sauce Hoisin
- 5 c. à soupe de sauce soja ou tamari
- 1 c. à thé de sauce chili sucrée
- 1 tasse de noix de cajou, hachées

Pour préparer les lits de laitue, séparer les feuilles externes de la tête de laitue, en prenant soin de ne pas briser les feuilles. Laver, sécher et disposer sur une assiette de service.

Hacher les poitrines de poulet en petits morceaux. Mettre de côté.

Dans une **Poêle de 11 po/28 cm de la Série ChefMC** avec couvercle, faire chauffer l'huile de sésame à feu moyen. Entretemps, hacher l'oignon, le gingembre et l'ail dans un **Rapido-chef**. Ajouter le mélange dans la poêle et cuire 5 minutes, jusqu'à ce que les légumes soient tendres. Ajouter le poulet, les noix de cajou, la sauce Hoisin, la sauce soja et la sauce chili. Remuer et cuire jusqu'à ce que le tout soit bien chauffé. Servir immédiatement sur les lits de laitue, ce qui permet à chacun d'assembler les roulés de laitue soi-même.

Valeur nutritive (par portion) : Calories : 300 Total lipides : 14 g Lipides saturés : 2,5 g Cholestérol : 40 g Glucides : 27 g Sucres : 13 g Fibres : 3 g Protéines : 20 g Sodium : 1490 mg Vitamine A : 10 % Vitamine C : 8 % Calcium : 6 % Fer : 15 %

Donne 8 portions

Le pesto frais dans cette salade fait toute la différence, en ajoutant une profondeur noisetée et une couleur verdoyante à la salade. Faites-le un jour à l'avance pour donner aux saveurs le temps de s'harmoniser.

salade d'orzo aux épinards tendres

Pesto (voir page 112)
Vinaigrette au pesto (voir page 112)
2 tasse de pâtes orzo non cuites
2 tasses de poulet cuit (soit dans **l'Intelli-Vap Tupperware®** ou rôti)
8 oz/225 g de tomates cerises
6 oz/170 g de jeunes épinards, lavés
2–3 c. à soupe de Parmesan
sel et poivre

Porter 2 pintes/1,8 L d'eau salée à ébullition dans une **Casserole de 3 pt/2,8 L de la Série ChefMC**. Ajouter les pâtes orzo et cuire 9 minutes ou al dente. Égoutter les pâtes, remuer avec les épinards, le poulet, les tomates et la Vinaigrette au pesto. Ajouter du Parmesan, du sel et du poivre au goût.

Valeur nutritive (par portion) : Calories : 430 Total lipides : 24 g Lipides saturés : 4 g Cholestérol : 35 mg Glucides : 34 g Sucres : 3 g Fibres : 2 g Protéines :19 g Sodium : 105 mg Vitamine A : 50 % Vitamine C : 15 % Calcium : 8 % Fer : 15 %

Donne 4 portions

Le quinoa est une céréale du Pérou qui a une texture semblable à celle du couscous. Il est disponible dans la plupart des épiceries et constitue une façon délicieuse d'ajouter des céréales complètes à votre régime alimentaire.

salade quinoa et longe de porc

2 lb/1 kg de longe de porc
5,6 oz/160 g de quinoa nature, non cuit
½ tasse de coeurs d'artichauts, tranchés, marinés
¼ tasse d'olives tranchées
½ botte de jeunes épinards frais
1 tasse de tomates cerises, coupées en deux
2 c. à soupe de persil à feuilles plates, finement haché
¼ tasse de vinaigre balsamique
1 ½ c. à soupe d'huile d'olive extra vierge
4 gousses d'ail, émincé
sel et poivre

Verser de l'eau dans le réservoir de **l'Intelli-Vap Tupperware®**. Mettre la longe de porc dans le bol étuveur. Cuire aux micro-ondes sur Fort pendant 17 minutes, ou jusqu'à ce que le porc atteigne une température interne de 165 °F/75 °C. Laissez reposer 5 minutes, puis trancher finement.

Préparer le quinoa dans le **Cuit-riz micro-ondes de Tupperware®** selon les instructions du feuillet descriptif du produit. Laisser refroidir et aérer le quinoa avec une cuiller de service. Ajouter les coeurs d'artichauts, les olives, les épinards, les tomates cerises et le persil. Dans un petit bol, fouetter ensemble le vinaigre balsamique, l'huile d'olive et l'ail jusqu'à ce que le tout soit bien mélangé; assaisonner de sel et de poivre au goût et verser sur la salade. Remuer pour combiner.

Valeur nutritive (par portion) : Calories : 620 Total lipides : 26 g Lipides saturés : 6 g Cholestérol : 150 mg Glucides : 36 g Sucres : 7 g Fibres : 5 g Protéines : 57 g Sodium : 290 mg Vitamine A : 90 % Vitamine C : 40 % Calcium : 10 % Fer : 35 %

Donne 4 portions

Savourez un arôme Tex-Mex piquant dans cette salade mexicaine que toute la famille appréciera.

salade de poulet santa fe avec quesadillas

10 oz/285 g de salade mélangée en sachet
15 oz/425 g de haricots noirs en boîte, égouttés
1 tasse de maïs congelé
2 poitrines de poulet
1 c. à thé d'huile végétale
4 tortillas à la farine de 8 po/20 cm
1 tasse de fromage cheddar fort, en lamelles
½ tasse de Vinaigrette coriandre-lime (voir page 111)
sel et poivre

Dans **l'Intelli-Vap Tupperware®**, mettre le poulet dans le bol étuveur et le maïs congelé dans la passoire. Remplir le réservoir avec 1 ½ tasse/ 400 mL d'eau. Cuire aux micro-ondes sur Fort pendant 15 minutes, ou jusqu'à ce que le poulet soit bien cuit. Quand il est suffisamment refroidi pour le manipuler, le trancher finement. Mettre de côté.

Faire chauffer l'huile végétale dans une **Poêle de 8 po/20 cm de la Série Chef^MC** à feu moyen. Mettre ¼ tasse de fromage sur chaque tortilla. Plier la tortilla en deux et la mettre dans la poêle; en cuire plusieurs à la fois. Cuire 2 minutes de chaque côté, jusqu'à ce que le fromage soit fondu et que l'extérieur de la tortilla soit rissolé. Mettre de côté et tenir au chaud.

Dans un bol de service, mêler la verdure, le maïs, les haricots, le poulet et la vinaigrette préparée. Garnir de quesadillas. Servir immédiatement.

Valeur nutritive (par portion) : Calories : 540 Total lipides : 24 g Lipides saturés : 8 g Cholestérol : 65 mg Glucides : 51 g Sucres : 4 g Fibres : 8 g Protéines : 30 g Sodium : 1520 mg Vitamine A : 60 % Vitamine C : 8 % Calcium : 25 % Fer : 80 %

Donne 4 portions

Faites comme si vous alliez dans votre grilladerie préférée en préparant cette salade facile et délicieuse. Ce plat principal copieux satisfera à coup sûr même les gros appétits.

salade style grilladerie

2 biftecks de filet mignon de 4 oz/115 g
2 gros champignons Portobello, tranchés
1 c. à thé d'huile végétale
10 oz/265 g de salade mélangée en sachet
½ tasse de Vinaigrette vin rouge à la framboise (voir page 112)
½ tasse de miettes de fromage bleu
½ tasse de poivrons rouges grillés en bocal, égouttés et tranchés
sel et poivre

Dans une **Poêle de 11 po/28 cm de la Série Chef^MC**, faire chauffer l'huile à feu moyen. Assaisonner les biftecks de sel et poivre, et mettre ensuite dans la poêle très chaude, pour saisir pendant 6 minutes de chaque côté ou jusqu'à ce que les steaks atteignent le degré de cuisson désiré. Retirer les steaks et laisser reposer sur une planche à découper 5 minutes. Cuire les champignons dans l'huile chaude jusqu'à ce qu'ils soient tendres. Retirer les champignons. Découper la viande en tranches minces. Tenir au chaud.

Pour assembler la salade, mettre la verdure dans un grand bol à salade. Remuer avec la vinaigrette. Garnir avec la viande, les champignons, les poivrons et le fromage. Servir immédiatement.

Valeur nutritive (par portion) : Calories : 410 Total lipides : 35 g Lipides saturés : 9 g Cholestérol : 50 mg Glucides : 9 g Sucres : 4 g Fibres : 3 g Protéines : 17 g Sodium : 410 mg Vitamine A : 60 % Vitamine C : 15 % Calcium : 10 % Fer :10 %

Donne 4 portions

Cette salade d'inspiration asiatique combine tout ce qui fait l'intérêt des aliments asiatiques : sucré, salé, aigre et copieux. Le saumon est rempli de graisses monoinsaturées qui vous maintiennent en bonne santé et abaissent le cholestérol.

saumon vapeur et chou asiatique

1 lb/455 g de filet de saumon
Chou nappa de 2 lb
1 botte d'oignons verts
1 pqt de nouilles Ramen
1 pqt d'amandes effilées
3 c. à soupe de beurre
sel et poivre
Vinaigrette aigre-douce (voir page 112)

Cuire le saumon à la vapeur pendant 10 minutes dans **l'Intelli-Vap Tupperware®** jusqu'à ce qu'il soit opaque. Hacher menu le chou et trancher les oignons verts; mettre dans un grand bol. Faire chauffer le beurre dans une **Poêle de 11 po/ 28 cm de la Série Chef[MC]** à feu moyen. Écraser les nouilles et les ajouter avec les amandes au beurre fondu. Cuire jusqu'à ce que le mélange soit rissolé. Bien égoutter et mettre de côté. Juste avant de servir, ajouter au chou les nouilles et les amandes et remuer avec la vinaigrette. Recouvrir avec le saumon vapeur.

Valeur nutritive (par portion) : Calories : 920 Total lipides : 63 g Lipides saturés : 10 g Cholestérol : 95 mg Glucides : 56 g Sucres : 30 g Fibres : 9 g Protéines : 38 g Sodium : 310 mg Vitamine A : 60 % Vitamine C : 110 % Calcium : 30 % Fer : 15 %

Donne 4 portions

Les herbes aromatiques et les légumes croquants donnent du mordant à cette salade. Ajoutez des segments de mandarine pour un goût édulcoré.

salade thaï de boeuf et tofu

12 oz/340 g de tofu extra ferme
6 tasses de mélange printanier
½ tasse de menthe fraîche
½ tasse de basilic frais
1 gros concombre, pelé et finement tranché
1 oignon rouge, en quartiers
1 c. à soupe d'huile d'arachide
8 oz/225 g de bifteck de hampe ou de flanc, paré
8 oz/225 g de segments de mandarine en boîte, égouttés
set et poivre
Vinaigrette thaï (voir page 112)

Garnir une assiette de serviettes en papier. Sortir le tofu de l'emballage, l'égoutter et le couper en cubes de 1 pouce. Les disposer sur les serviettes en papier et laisser égoutter 30 minutes. Exprimer doucement le liquide restant à l'aide de serviettes en papier.

Dans un **Rapido-chef** avec la lame, combiner l'oignon et le concombre et tourner la manivelle pour hacher grossièrement. Dans un grand bol, combiner la laitue, la menthe, le basilic et le mélange de concombre. Verser la moitié de la vinaigrette sur le mélange de laitue; remuer pour imbiber. Faire chauffer une **Poêle de 11 po / 28 cm de la Série Chef[MC]** à feu moyen. Ajouter l'huile d'arachide dans la poêle. Ajouter le boeuf et cuire 3 minutes de chaque côté, ou jusqu'à ce que la viande atteigne le degré désiré de cuisson. Retirer la viande de la poêle et laisser reposer 5 minutes sur une planche à découper. Ajouter le tofu dans la poêle chaude. Cuire le tofu jusqu'à ce qu'il soit légèrement rissolé. Retirer du feu et mettre de côté. Trancher finement le boeuf et le mettre dans le bol avec le mélange de salade. Ajouter le tofu; remuer pour combiner. Garnir de segments de mandarine.

Note : Remplacer le boeuf par du saumon ou du poulet cuits à la vapeur.

Valeur nutritive (par portion) : Calories : 270 Total lipides : 15 g Lipides saturés : 2,5 g Cholestérol : 30 mg Glucides : 15 g Sucres : 7 g Fibres : 4 g Protéines : 22 g Sodium : 400 mg Vitamine A : 35 % Vitamine C : 45 % Calcium : 25 % Fer : 25 %

Donne 4 portions

La salade Hollywood (californienne ou Cobb) classique est une des meilleures. Servie en plat principal, elle combine tous les accompagnements classiques avec une divine vinaigrette au vinaigre de champagne.

salade hollywood à la dinde

- 2 c. à soupe de vinaigre de champagne
- 2 c. à thé de moutarde de Dijon
- 1 c. à thé de sauce Worcestershire
- ½ tasse de mayonnaise légère
- ¼ tasse d'huile d'olive extra vierge
- 4 oz/115 g de fromage bleu émietté
- ¾ tasse ou 6 tranches de bacon pré-cuit, émietté
- 10 oz/285 g de mélange printanier
- 1 petit avocat, épluché, dénoyauté et en tranches
- 4 petites tomates, hachées
- ½ lb de poitrine de dinde, en cubes
- sel et poivre

Dans la base du **Batteur Gagne-temps**, mettre le vinaigre de champagne, la moutarde de Dijon, la sauce Worcestershire, la mayonnaise et l'huile d'olive. Remettre le couvercle et tourner la manivelle pour mélanger parfaitement. Mettre de côté. Mettre le bacon sur une assiette pour micro-ondes et faire chauffer aux micro-ondes 1 minute jusqu'à ce qu'il soit croustillant. Émietter et mettre de côté. Mettre le mélange printanier dans un grand bol. Disposer le bacon, l'avocat, les tomates et la dinde sur le dessus. Arroser de vinaigrette et servir.

Note : Pour une présentation traditionnelle, disposer les avocats, les tomates, la dinde et le bacon en rang sur la verdure.

Valeur nutritive (par portion) : Calories : 540 Total lipides : 45 g Lipides saturés : 11 g Cholestérol : 65 mg Glucides : 18 g Sucres : 7 g Fibres : 6 g Protéines : 22 g Sodium : 1420 mg Vitamine A : 45 % Vitamine C : 35 % Calcium : 20 % Fer :10 %

Donne 6 portions

La salade de thon peut être délicieuse sans être riche. Cette version allégée met à l'honneur des haricots blancs et des légumes croquants pour une parfaite combinaison de croquant-crémeux.

salade de thon toscane

- 6 oz/170 g de thon blanc en boîte, égoutté
- 15 oz/425 g de haricots blancs en boîte, égouttés et rincés
- 2 tiges de céleri
- ½ oignon rouge, en quartiers
- ½ tasse de persil
- ¾ tasse de Vinaigrette au vin rouge (voir page 112)
- sel et poivre

Mettre le céleri, l'oignon et le persil dans la base du **Hachoir Gagne-temps**. Tirer la corde 4-5 fois pour hacher finement. Combiner ce mélange avec le reste des ingrédients dans un grand bol. Ajouter le sel et le poivre au goût. Servir immédiatement ou réfrigérer pendant trois jours maximum.

Valeur nutritive (par portion) : Calories : 250 Total lipides : 19 g Lipides saturés : 2,5 g Cholestérol : 10 mg Glucides : 12 g Sucres : 2 g Fibres : 3 g Protéines : 11 g Sodium : 230 mg Vitamine A : 10 % Vitamine C : 15 % Calcium : 4 % Fer : 8 %

salades pour des enfants heureux, en pleine santé

Vos petits trésors adoreront les délicieuses salades amusantes incluses dans cette section. Conçues à l'intention des enfants, elles sont remplies de choses qu'ils aiment déjà. Ils ne sauront pas que ces plats sont également pleins de fruits et légumes sains pour une bonne croissance. Ce sont des salades qui les rassasieront et leur laisseront le sourire aux lèvres.

salade baseball

Votre petit cogneur adorera cette façon amusante de manger le mets préféré des joueurs de baseball—des hot dogs! Pour une version moins grasse, optez pour les hot dogs à la dinde.

Donne 6 portions

¼ tasse de ketchup
¼ tasse de mayonnaise à faible teneur en gras
¼ tasse de relish sucrée
1 c. à soupe de moutarde à grain entiers
1 c. à thé d'huile végétale
6 hot dogs, coupés en tranches de 1 pouce
8 oz/225 g de mélange pour salade de chou, en sachet
10 oz/285 g de laitue mélangée, en sachet
4 petites tomates mûries sur pied, en dés
½ tasse de cornichons, en dés
sel et poivre

Dans la base du **Batteur Gagne-temps**, mettre le ketchup, la mayonnaise, la relish et la moutarde. Remettre le couvercle et tourner la manivelle pour mélanger parfaitement. Mettre de côté ou réfrigérer si on ne l'utilise pas immédiatement.

Faire chauffer l'huile végétale dans une **Poêle de 11 po/28 cm de la Série Chef^{MC}** à feu moyen. Ajouter les morceaux de hot dogs et cuire pendant cinq minutes, ou jusqu'à ce que les hot dogs soient bien cuits.

Dans un bol de service, remuer la laitue, le mélange de salade de chou, les tomates, les condiments et la vinaigrette préparée. Garnir avec les morceaux de hot dogs. Servir immédiatement.

Valeur nutritive (par portion) : Calories : 240
Total lipides : 18 g Lipides saturés : 6 g
Cholestérol : 30 mg Glucides : 15 g
Sucres : 10 g Fibres : 2 g
Protéines : 16 g
Sodium : 890 mg
Vitamine A : 30 %
Vitamine C : 40 %
Calcium : 4 % Fer : 6 %

salade crémeuse de macaroni ranch

Alternative légère et plus équilibrée aux "mac" au fromage, cette salade de pâtes incorpore une vinaigrette Ranch et des pâtes dont les enfants adoreront la forme.

Donne 8 portions

8 oz/225 g de pâtes en roues de wagon ou autres petites pâtes, non cuites
1 lb/455 g de légumes mélangés congelés
1 petit poivron rouge, en quartiers
2 tasses de poulet (cuit dans **l'Intelli-Vap Tupperware®** ou de rôtisserie), coupé en dés
Vinaigrette Ranch légère (voir page 112)
sel et poivre noir

Mettre les légumes congelés dans le bol étuveur de **l'Intelli-Vap Tupperware®**. Cuire aux micro-ondes sur Fort pendant 10 minutes. Retirer le bol étuveur et rincer les légumes à l'eau froide pour arrêter la cuisson. Porter 2 L d'eau salée à ébullition dans une **Casserole de 2,8 L/3 pt de la Série Chef[MC]**. Ajouter les pâtes et cuire 9 minutes ou jusqu'à ce que les pâtes soient al dente. Égoutter les pâtes et rincer à l'eau froide jusqu'à ce qu'elles soient complètement froides. Mettre les poivrons rouges dans la base du **Hachoir Gagne-temps**. Remettre le couvercle et tirer sur la corde 2–3 fois pour hacher grossièrement. Mettre les pâtes, le poulet, les légumes et le poivron rouge dans un grand bol. Remuer avec la vinaigrette, le sel et le poivre noir au goût.

Valeur nutritive (par portion) : Calories : 260
Total lipides : 6 g Lipides saturés : 2 g Cholestérol : 40 mg
Glucides : 32 g Sucres : 5 g Fibres : 2 g Protéines : 17 g
Sodium : 120 mg Vitamine A : 30 % Vitamine C : 30 %
Calcium : 6 % Fer : 8 %

salade de petites croquettes de poulet

Au lieu des frites, servez à vos enfants des croquettes de poulet sur une salade de confetti amusante composée de laitue en lamelles et de cheddar. Une vinaigrette légère et piquante fera de cette salade un succès.

Donne 6 portions

½ tasse de mayonnaise légère
2 c. à soupe de miel
2 c. à soupe de moutarde jaune
2 c. à soupe de jus de citron
8 oz/225 g de laitue en lamelles style taco, en sachet
8 oz/225 g de mélange de chou, en sachet
1 tasse de mini-bretzels durs
1 tasse de fromage cheddar en lamelles
1 tasse de tomates raisins, coupées en deux
6 doigts de poulet panés préparés, coupés en morceaux
sel et poivre

Dans la base du **Batteur Gagne-temps**, mettre la mayonnaise, le miel, la moutarde et le jus de citron. Remettre le couvercle et tourner la manivelle pour mélanger parfaitement. Mettre de côté ou réfrigérer, si on ne l'utilise pas immédiatement. Dans un grand bol, combiner la laitue, le mélange de salade de chou et la vinaigrette préparée. Garnir avec les bretzels, le fromage, les tomates et le poulet. Servir immédiatement.

Note : Les doigts de poulet peuvent être achetés dans la section déli ou avec les aliments-minute dans la section réfrigérée ou congélation de votre magasin.

Valeur nutritive (par portion) : Calories : 350
Total lipides : 20 g Lipides saturés : 6 g
Cholestérol : 50 mg Glucides : 26 g
Sucres : 10 g Fibres : 3 g Protéines : 18 g
Sodium : 770 mg Vitamine A : 15 %
Vitamine C : 40 % Calcium : 15 % Fer : 6 %

salade délices à l'orange

Voici un mets sucré-acidulé pour régaler toute la famille. Gorgée de vitamines A & C, cette salade aidera vos enfants à développer une bonne vue et des os sains.

Donne 4 portions

10 oz/285 g de bâtonnets de carottes en sachet *ou* de carottes râpées avec la **Râpe-À-mesure**
1 tasse de canneberges déshydratées
1 c. à soupe de graines de pavot
8 oz/225 g de morceaux d'ananas et jus (en boîte)
½ tasse de jus d'orange
sel et poivre

Mettre les bâtonnets ou les carottes râpées dans la base du **Rapido-chef** et tourner la manivelle pour hacher rapidement en petits morceaux. Combiner tous les ingrédients dans un bol de service. Réfrigérer plusieurs heures pour que les arômes se développent. Servir froid.

Valeur nutritive (par portion) : Calories : 180
Total lipides : 1,5 g Lipides saturés : 0 g Cholestérol : 0 mg
Glucides : 43 g Sucres : 32 g Fibres : 5 g Protéines : 1 g
Sodium : 55 mg Vitamine A : 240 % Vitamine C : 45 %
Calcium : 6 % Fer : 4 %

vinaigrettes

Une vinaigrette fraîche est facile, sans agent de conservation et amusante à faire. Que ce soit une vinaigrette ranch crémeuse ou une vinaigrette piquante, confectionner votre propre vinaigrette à la maison vous fera économiser de l'argent et ajoutera une saveur fraîche à vos créations de salade. La saveur et l'inspiration culturelle de ces vinaigrettes varient. Utilisez votre imagination pour combiner les vinaigrettes et les salades pour un profil de saveurs différent à chaque fois.

vinaigrette au basilic

Donne ½ tasse

½ tasse de feuilles de basilic frais
2 c. à soupe de vinaigre balsamique
1 c. à soupe de miel
½ tasse d'huile d'olive
sel et poivre

Mettre les feuilles de basilic frais dans la base du **Hachoir Gagne-temps**. Tirer sur la corde 4–5 fois pour hacher. Mettre le basilic, le vinaigre balsamique, le miel, l'huile d'olive, le sel et le poivre dans un **Mélangeur rapide.** Remettre le couvercle et agiter jusqu'à ce que le tout soit bien incorporé.

Valeur nutritive (par portion) : Calories : 280
Total lipides : 28 g Lipides saturés : 4 g
Cholestérol : 0 mg Glucides : 6 g
Sucres : 6 g Fibres : 0 g Protéines : 0 g
Sodium : 0 mg

vinaigrette coriandre-lime

Donne 2 tasses

1 tasse de bouillon de légumes
1 ½ c. à thé de fécule d'arrow-root ou de maïs
½ tasse de jus de lime frais
½ c. à thé de sucre
2 c. à soupe d'huile de sésame
¼ tasse d'huile d'arachide
2 c. à soupe d'huile de canola
2 c. à soupe de sel marin
1 c. à thé de coriandre

Combiner l'arrow-root avec 1 ½ c. à thé de bouillon froid et mélanger pour former une pâte. Porter le reste du bouillon à ébullition dans une petite casserole et ajouter en remuant la pâte d'arrow-root. Porter à ébullition jusqu'à épaississement, environ 2 minutes. Retirer du feu et refroidir. Ajouter le jus de lime et le sucre; remuer pour combiner. Refroidir complètement au réfrigérateur ou dans un bol posé sur de la glace. Mettre le mélange refroidi dans un **Mélangeur rapide.** Ajouter l'huile, remettre le couvercle et bien agiter pour mélanger. Ajouter le sel et la coriandre.

Valeur nutritive (par portion) : Calories : 70
Total lipides : 7 g Lipides saturés : 1 g
Cholestérol : 0 mg Glucides : 1 g
Sucres : 1 g Fibres : 0 g Protéines : 0 g
Sodium : 710 mg

vinaigrette grecque

Donne ½ tasse

4 c. à soupe de jus de citron
2 gousses d'ail, hachées
¼ tasse d'huile d'olive extra vierge

Ajouter tous les ingrédients dans un **Mélangeur rapide.** Remettre le couvercle et agiter jusqu'à ce que le tout soit bien combiné.

Valeur nutritive (par portion) : Calories : 130
Total lipides : 14 g Lipides saturés : 2 g
Cholestérol : 0 mg Glucides : 2 mg
Sucres : 0 mg Fibres : 0 g Protéines : 0 g
Sodium : 0 mg

vinaigrette miel-moutarde

Donne ¾ tasse

½ tasse de mayonnaise légère
2 c. à soupe de miel
2 c. à soupe de moutarde jaune
2 c. à soupe de jus de citron
sel et poivre

Dans la base du **Batteur Gagne-temps**, mettre la mayonnaise, le miel, la moutarde, le jus de citron et les assaisonnements. Remettre le couvercle et tourner la manivelle pour bien mélanger.

Valeur nutritive (par portion) : Calories : 80
Total lipides : 6 g Lipides saturés : 1 g
Cholestérol : 5 mg Glucides : 7 g
Sucres : 6 g Fibres : 0 g Protéines : 0 g
Sodium : 160 mg

vinaigrette légère style ranch
Donne ¾ tasse

½ tasse de babeurre
½ tasse de crème sure légère
¼ tasse de mayonnaise légère
1 c. à soupe de jus de citron
1 c. à soupe de ciboulette
1 gousse d'ail
sel et poivre

Mettre l'ail et la ciboulette dans le bol du **Hachoir Gagne-temps**. Remettre le couvercle et tirer sur la corde 4–5 fois pour hacher finement. Mettre le babeurre, la crème sure, la mayonnaise dans la base du **Batteur Gagne-temps**. Avec le **Presse citron-lime Tupperware®**, extraire le jus de citron dans le contenant, ajouter l'ail et la ciboulette. Remettre le couvercle, tourner la manivelle pour mélanger parfaitement.

Valeur nutritive (par portion) : Calories : 35
Total lipides : 3 g Lipides saturés : 1 g
Cholestérol : 5 mg Glucides : 2 g Sucres : 1 g
Fibres : 0 g Protéines : 1 g Sodium : 40 mg

vinaigrette à l'arachide
Donne 1 ⅛ tasse

¼ tasse, plus 1 c. à soupe de beurre d'arachide entièrement naturel ou fraîchement moulu
2 c. à soupe de miel
1 c. à thé de sauce soja
¼ tasse de vinaigre de riz
¼ tasse d'huile de canola
1 c. à soupe d'huile de sésame
2 c. à soupe d'eau chaude
sel et poivre

Combiner tous les ingrédients dans la base du **Batteur Gagne-temps**. Remettre le couvercle et mélanger jusqu'à ce que le tout soit homogène. Garder au réfrigérateur jusqu'à 1 semaine.

Valeur nutritive (par portion) : Calories : 130
Total lipides : 12 g Lipides saturés : 1,5 g
Cholestérol : 0 mg Glucides : 6 g Sucres : 5 g
Fibres : 1 g Protéines : 2 g Sodium : 80 mg

vinaigrette au pesto
Donne ¾ tasse

⅔ tasse de pesto préparé
2 c. à soupe de vinaigre de vin blanc
3 c. à soupe d'huile d'olive extra vierge
sel et poivre

Mettre le pesto, le vinaigre, le sel et le poivre dans un **Mélangeur rapide**. Ajouter l'huile d'olive, remettre le couvercle et agiter jusqu'à ce que les ingrédients soient bien incorporés.

Valeur nutritive (par portion) : Calories : 210
Total lipides : 22 g Lipides saturés : 3,5 g
Cholestérol : 0 mg Glucides : 1 g Sucres : 0 g
Fibres : 0 g Protéines : 2 g Sodium : 40 mg

pesto
Donne ⅔ tasse

¾ tasse de feuilles de basilic tassées
3 c. à soupe de pignons, grillés
1 gousse d'ail
¼ tasse de fromage Parmesan râpé
½ tasse d'huile d'olive extra vierge
sel et poivre

Mettre le basilic, les pignons, l'ail, le fromage Parmesan et l'huile dans la base du **Hachoir Gagne-temps**. Remettre le couvercle, tourner pour fermer hermétiquement et tirer sur la corde 4–5 fois jusqu'à ce que le mélange soit finement haché. Assaisonner de sel et de poivre.

Valeur nutritive (par portion) : Calories : 160
Total lipides : 17 g Lipides saturés : 2,5 g
Cholestérol : 0 mg Glucides : 1 g Sucres : 0 g
Fibres : 0 g Protéines : 2 g Sodium : 40 mg

vinaigrette aux graines de pavot
Donne ¾ tasse

½ tasse de mayonnaise
2 c. à soupe de miel
½ c. à soupe de moutarde de Dijon
1 c. à soupe de vinaigre de cidre de pomme
2 c. à soupe de jus de citron
½ c. à soupe de graines de pavot
sel et poivre

Ajouter tous les ingrédients dans la base du **Mélangeur rapide**. Remettre le couvercle et agiter jusqu'à ce que le tout soit bien combiné.

Valeur nutritive (par portion) : Calories : 90
Total lipides : 7 g Lipides saturés : 1 g
Cholestérol : 5 mg Glucides : 8 g Sucres : 7 g
Fibres : 0 g Protéines : 0 g Sodium : 260 mg

vinaigrette de vin rouge à la framboise
Donne 1 tasse

¼ tasse de vinaigre de vin rouge à la framboise
¾ tasse d'huile d'olive
1 c. à thé de moutarde de Dijon
2 gousses d'ail, émincées
sel et poivre

Ajouter tous les ingrédients dans un **Mélangeur rapide**. Remettre le couvercle et agiter jusqu'à ce que le tout soit bien combiné.

Valeur nutritive (par portion) : Calories : 190
Total lipides : 21 g Lipides saturés : 3 g
Cholestérol : 0 mg Glucides : 0 g Sucres : 0 g
Fibres : 0 g Protéines : 0 g Sodium : 15 mg

vinaigrette au vin rouge
Donne ¾ tasse

¼ tasse de vinaigre de vin rouge
2 c. à soupe de jus de citron
1 c. à thé de miel
½ tasse d'huile d'olive extra vierge
sel et poivre

Ajouter tous les ingrédients dans un **Mélangeur rapide**. Remettre le couvercle et agiter jusqu'à ce que le tout soit bien combiné.

Valeur nutritive (par portion) : Calories : 170
Total lipides : 19 g Lipides saturés : 2,5 g
Cholestérol : 0 mg Glucides : 1 g Sucres : 1 g
Fibres : 0 g Protéines : 0 g Sodium : 0 mg

vinaigrette revigorante
Donne 1 ⅛ tasse

½ c. à thé de poivre de cayenne
¼ tasse de vinaigre de vin blanc
1 c. à thé de sel
1 c. à thé de moutarde en poudre
2 ½ c. à thé de sucre
1 c. à thé de poudre d'ail
10–12 gouttes de sauce au piment fort
¾ tasse d'huile végétale

Combiner tous les ingrédients, sauf l'huile végétale, dans un **Mélangeur rapide**. Agiter vigoureusement jusqu'à ce que le tout soit combiné. Retirer le couvercle à capuchon, ajouter l'huile végétale, remettre le couvercle et agiter jusqu'à ce que le tout soit bien incorporé.

Valeur nutritive (par portion) : Calories : 170
Total lipides : 18 g Lipides saturés : 1,5 g
Cholestérol : 0 mg Glucides : 2 g Sucres : 1 g
Fibres : 0 g Protéines : 0 g Sodium : 270 mg

vinaigrette aigre-douce
Donne 1 tasse

½ tasse d'huile de canola
½ tasse de sucre
¼ tasse de vinaigre de cidre de pomme
sel et poivre

Mettre tous les ingrédients dans un **Mélangeur rapide**. Remettre le couvercle et bien agiter jusqu'à ce que le tout soit bien combiné.

Valeur nutritive (par portion) : Calories : 140
Total lipides : 11 g Lipides saturés : 1 g
Cholestérol : 0 mg Glucides : 10 g Sucres : 10 g
Fibres : 0 g Protéines : 0 g Sodium : 60 mg

vinaigrette thaï
Donne ⅓ tasse

½ piment jalapeno, épépiné
¼ tasse de jus de lime
1 c. à soupe de sauce au poisson Thaï
2 c. à thé d'huile de sésame
½ c. à thé de sucre

Hacher finement le piment jalapeno avec le **Couteau tout usage de la Série Chef^MC Pro**. Ajouter le piment jalapeno, la lime, la sauce au poisson, l'huile de sésame et le sucre dans un **Mélangeur rapide**. Remettre le couvercle et secouer jusqu'à ce que le tout soit bien combiné.

Valeur nutritive (par portion) : Calories : 30
Total lipides : 2,5 g Lipides saturés : 0 g
Cholestérol : 0 mg Glucides : 2 g Sucres : 1 g
Fibres : 0 g Protéines : 0 g Sodium : 350 mg

The recipes that appear in this recipe book were written and developed by **Carol Stafford,** Global Culinary Chef for Tupperware Brands Corporation. Chef Carol received a B.S. in Food and Nutrition from Florida International University in Miami, Florida. In 2009, she received ProChef certification from the Culinary Institute of America in Hyde Park, New York.

Las recetas que aparecen en este libro de recetas fueron escritas y desarrolladas por **Carol Stafford**, Chef de Artes Culinarias de la división Global de la Corporación Tupperware Brands. Chef Carol cuenta con un Bachillerato en Ciencias (B.S.) en Nutrición y Alimentación de la Universidad Internacional de Florida, ubicada en Miami. En el 2009, recibió una certificación ProChef del Instituto Culinario de América en Hyde Park, Nueva York.

Les recettes qui apparaissent dans ce livre de recettes ont été élaborées par **Carol Stafford**, Chef de cuisine pour Tupperware Brands Corporation. Chef Carol a reçu un Baccalauréat ès Sciences alimentaires et Nutrition de l'université internationale de Floride à Miami. En 2009, elle a reçu l'accréditation de ProChef du Culinary Institute of America à Hyde Park, New York.